Voices of Cork

The Knitting Map Speaks

Voices of Cork

The Knitting Map Speaks

Kieran McCarthy

NONSUCH

Dedicated to the great community of The Knitting Map for

sharing your great spirit and kindness.

Also to my Nan, Alice, for showing me that home

is where the heart is.

First published 2005

Nonsuch Publishing Limited
73 Lower Leeson Street
Dublin 2
Ireland

www.nonsuchireland.com

National Library Cataloguing in Publication Data.
A catalogue record for this book is available from the National Library.

ISBN 1 84588 522 8

Typesetting and origination by Tempus Publishing Limited.
Printed in Great Britain.

Contents

About The Author   7

Acknowledgements   8

Picture credits   8

half/angel   9

The Knitting Map: 10

Foreword: Falling and Flying   11

Preface: Voices of a European Capital of Culture   13

Chapter 1: The Knitting Map as a Revolution   19

  Kate O' Brien: How Do You Start a Revolution?   19

  Mercy Foley: Labour of Love   21

  Betty Flynn: Beyond Vision   23

  Caroline Kearney: I like Knitting   26

  Marion O' Sullivan: People Can Talk… Make Friends… Learn to knit   27

  Ena Atkinson: Knitting is History. It Has Been Around a Long Time   28

  Sr Kathleen Hopkins: It's a Gift for the Area   29

  Teresa Geary: We had Good Times and Bad Times   31

  Maureen McGrath: A Knitting Education   32

  Sr Mary Ryan: Make the most out of life   32

  Mel Murphy: Life is Too Short to Drink Bad Coffee   34

  Grace Madden: Enjoying the Map   35

  Enrika Bertolini Cullen: The Diamond in the Rough   36

Chapter 2: Growing Up and Family Life   39

  Ann Ralph: I Promise to be as Good as Gold   39

  Sally Buckley: It was a very simple time but we were very happy   40

  Rose Conlon: Be Optimistic, Not Pessimistic   42

  Jane Duggan: A True Corkonian!   44

  Mary O' Driscoll & Teresa Hallahan (sisters, née Cummins): Blackrock: A Fishing Story   46

  Dolores Cummins: Cork: Capital of Activity   48

  Liam McCarthy: A King's Lifestyle on a Pauper's Budget   49

  Kay Mulcahy: With life, the glass is always half full   52

  Stella Barry: Unchained Melodies   52

  Ciara Murphy: I Don't Have a Title to My Story   54

  Marion Sheehan: Rhythms of Life   55

Eithne Farr: Glimpses into the Past 56
Kay O' Riordan: How Lucky I am in Life 57
Rachel O' Mahony: Past, Present and Future 59
Katrina Forde: I Did it My Way 60
Fergal Crowley: Survival 61
Theresa Kelleher: My Faith 63

Chapter 3: The Architecture of Life 65
Barbara A. Bruen: Living Memories 65
Margaret O' Rourke: Back to Front: Three Phases in a Life 68
Mary Goggin: A Dream…Shattered 71
Una Long: I Can Die Happy Now 72
Margaret Kingston: Mix and Match 75
Jackie Magnin: Finding a Home 77
Elizabeth O' Dea: A Working Title 79
Margaret Kennedy: Keeping the Knots Unravelled 81
Eileen Henrick: Misadventures of Eileen Henrick 83
Francis McCarthy: And What I am Going to do Tomorrow? 85
Sally O' Neill: Pride of my Life 86
Anon.: A Hard Time In Life 88
Paula O' Callaghan: Be Happy Whatever you Take Up in Life 89
Loretta Mullins McGillion: Live It! 90
Judith Mtifukanji: Malawian Mai in Cork 90
Valerie O' Brien: What's meant to be, Will be 93
Sinead Barry: Go with the Flow 95
Mona Lucey: Get Along with People 95
Kit Deeney: Kindness is the basis of life 97

Chapter 4: Negotiating the Rhythms of Life 99
Maura O' Connell: In Search of Tranquillity 99
Margaret Jones: Guiding Travels 101
Clare Sands: Roar! 103
Elsie O' Connell: I had a very happy childhood 104
Anon: There'll be a piece of paper that will cause an awful lot of trouble 105
Louise Kiely: You'll Find Englishmen are Gentlemen 105
Lionel Powell: Striving to Improve Self 107
Margaret O' Sullivan: Everything Really is Larger than Life 108
Nokuthula Nkomo: We Talk … We Find Out About Different Cultures 110
Marilyn Munza: Believe in Yourself 111
Marie Foy Twomey: A Walk in the Countryside 112
Maureen O' Sullivan: A Poet's Escape 114
Rita Guinan: I'm their number one fan 116
Samantha Barry: Everything Happens For a Reason 117
Cynthia Kelly: Don't Take Life Too Seriously or You'll Never Get Out Alive 119
Sue Tector-Sands: This Ain't no Dress Rehearsal, This is the Real Thing 120
Cork 2005 Team: The Box over the Bed 123

Appendix One: Stitch Patterns and The Knitting Map 126
Appendix Two: Rainbow of colours that represent a range of weather 127

About The Author

Kieran McCarthy is a born and bred Corkonian. He graduated from University College Cork in 1999 with a Joint Honours Bachelor of Arts Degree in Geography and Archaeology. Kieran has lectured widely on Cork's past in association with numerous institutions, in particular University College Cork, the Cork Education and Support Centre, the Vocational Educational Committee as well as various community associations within Cork City. In particular, Kieran has a keen interest in disseminating knowledge about the importance of local history in Cork's primary and post primary schools. Since 2003, he has annually co-ordinated the *Discover Cork: Schools' History Project*. He has been involved in the compilation of several television reports for R.T.E. on various aspects of Cork's history.

Kieran is particularly known for his local history column in *Inside Cork*, a weekly Cork newspaper, where he has been writing a series on the development of Cork City since October 1999. In addition to this extensive body of work, he has published four books: *Pathways Through Time - Historical Walking Trails of Cork City* (2001), *Cork: A Pictorial Journey* (2001), *Discover Cork* (2003) and *A Dream Unfolding, Portrait of Saint Patrick's Hospital* (2004). Kieran is currently working as a freelance historical consultant and is pursuing a Masters of Philosophy (M.Phil) in Geography in the University College Cork. He can be contacted at mccarthy_kieran@yahoo.com or 087 655 3389.

Kieran McCarthy

Acknowledgements

A book like this cannot be penned without the support, time and patience of numerous individuals. First and foremost, I would like to thank The Knitting Map staff: Jools Gilson-Ellis (Artistic Director), Richard Povall (Artistic Director), Sue Tector-Sands (Project Co-ordinator), Elizabeth O' Dea (Company Administrator), Kate O' Brien (Project Manager), Margaret Kennedy (Administrative Assistant), Marian O' Sullivan (Team Expert), Mel Murphy (Team Expert), Mary Norris (Team Expert), Betty Flynn (Team Expert) and Eileen Henrick (Team Expert). My thanks also to Sirdar, Cork City Council and Cork 2005 for their vision in making The Knitting Map a reality. Thanks to Sarah O' Connor with her team at Nonsuch Publishing for their vision and experience with this publication. A very special thank you to the great community of The Knitting Map for their warmth, time, patience, chat, support and most of all, for sharing their life experiences. I am forever grateful.

Kieran McCarthy
November 2005

Picture credits

Richard Povall, Jools Gilson-Ellis, Bernadette Sweeney, Kieran McCarthy, Kate O' Brien, The Knitting Map team and personal pictures of the interviewees.

half/angel

half/angel is an arts and performance production company based in Ireland and England. The name half angel comes from the name of a trapeze move. It was chosen because it's about learning to fall in order to fly. It's about the taking of risk in order to achieve another type of aspiration. The company was formed in 1995 by Jools Gilson-Ellis and Richard Povall. *half/angel* works across disciplines and sites, so we make performance for theatres as well as outdoor spaces and installations for galleries as well as site specific locations. We also work across a range of urban and rural contexts. These have included an urban dock, a rural headland, a university quadrangle and a community of knitters. This work always has a poetic sensibility, grounded in Jools' writing and elaborated through a decade of collaboration in embodied practices.

We have often worked with emerging technologies, but this has always been as a tool to investigate content/modes of interaction with our audience/visitors. We have sometimes been known as a dance company; our corporeal curiosity revels in the professional dancing body, but also lurches beyond it to other kinds of bodies and embodied contexts. We are a company that makes unsettling installation spaces (The Lios 2004), haunting and raucous dance theatre (The Secret Project 1999) as well as vast audacious projects, which resist conventional forms (The Knitting Map 2005). *half/angel* has been a resident company at STEIM (Amsterdam), Institute for Choreography & Dance (Cork) and The Banff Centre for the Arts (Canada). half/angel's research into performance environments which connect physical, vocal and sonic gestures has been critically as well as artistically important in the field of Performance Studies.

The Knitting Map:

The Knitting Map is a large-scale durational community textile installation, which involves several thousand volunteer knitters, as well as digital motion and weather-sensing technologies. The work was commissioned by the Executive of European Capital of Culture: Cork 2005 and brings together a company with ten years experience of making experimental performance and installation in theatres and galleries (*halflangel*), with what is fundamentally a community textile project. *The Knitting Map* makes connections between the ordinary and the ethereal, by making information about the busyness of Cork City translate into a knitting pattern knitted by 25 people, every day for a year. The colour of yarn is generated by the weather. This abstract collaborative textile is a document of Cork's year as City of Culture. It is a visionary and beautiful piece of work, which interrogates notions of community, as well as manual and digital technologies.

If you visited *The Knitting Map* in Cork in 2005, what you would have seen is a beautifully constructed curving amphitheatre, built into the crypt of Saint Luke's Church, Summerhill, Cork. On this structure are twenty knitting stations, each of which comprises a seat, a basket of wool and a computer screen hidden in a box in the wooden structure. When a volunteer knitter comes into the space, they take a station, look at the screen, (which shows an ordinary knitting pattern) and begins to knit. The pattern on this screen comes from two sources. In Cork city centre, there are four CCTV cameras on major civic buildings. They all look at the city and register how busy it is. In general, when the city is quieter, the patterns generated by the computer programme are simpler and when the city is busier, the stitches are more complex. We also have a weather station where we take multiple readings about the weather every day and this information is combined to generate colour. Across the floor, piling up as the months go by is yards and yards of knitting; great tumbles of cables and garters and honeycomb in the dusky hues of our palette.

Falling and Flying

Ten years ago when Richard and I were strangers and starting to work together for the first time, we began our collaboration through the making of the CD-ROM *mouthplace*. This involved generating images and texts and one of the ways we did this was to video material. The earliest of these sessions involved working with sewing needles and red thread. One of the images was of five needles held by their tips in my mouth. Many of the women interviewed in this book, I know, will think it a strange activity to be placing needles threaded with scarlet thread inside one's mouth! And yet, ten years later, they are part of the same conversation. In 1995, this was a musing on the ways in which textiles and textile practices are part of the same set of cultural processes, processes which define femininity. By this unsettling image, I am making a connection between an instrument of textile labour and the physical flesh of being feminine. Scratching at the surface for ten years, textiles compel me because I am enchanted by the complex choreography of them as practices, but also by the plural ways they are able to function as metaphors for something else and also because I continue to want to write and develop new myths, narratives, images and poetry based on them. They continue to compel me because there is something I do not understand about my own obsession.

So what happens when artists who have spent several decades in the art world making work primarily seen by audiences attuned to the vagaries of contemporary choreography and visual art, make a change, shift their arena. What happens when the stuff of metaphor is made material? What happens when fictional stories of communities of knitters become actual communities? Well what happens is *The Knitting Map*. This is a work, which was always an outrageous one – to knit with hundreds of volunteer knitters patterns and colours drawn from the city by new technologies and then to knit for a year. This was only ever a project that could have survived its rocky journey to realisation with the support of the hundreds of extraordinary women you will read about in this book.

These are women for whom knitting is a kind of loving meditation. These are women for whom knitting was once about having very little and where the clothing of a family was an ordinary and urgent necessity. These are women who have knitted their way out of depression, grief and abuse. These are women who knit now as an act of solidarity with the women of this city because they are seeking asylum from all kinds of Africa's and beyond and whose experiences of violence, murder, the loss of their children and other family members, mean that they understand what it means to lose everything that is familiar to them. These are women who come to *The Knitting Map*, not for the knitting, but for the laughter. These are women who tell the filthiest of stories and others that have made me choke back tears and wonder at my own gentle loving life. These are women who astonish me with their sheer extraordinary force of life, who walk into *The Knitting Map* on a weekly basis with a sense of ownership and intent that humbles me. These are women who knit. These are women who knit complexities of cables and honeycombs and lattices without even looking down. These are women whose mathematical choreography with two plastic sticks and a ball of wool is an un-thought thing.

In the afternoons and mornings that make up a year of knitting, when we sit and knit, when something settles and we begin to talk, everything slows. There is time to talk, gossip, rant, muse and long. There is time. *The Knitting Map* is a choreography of time, conjured out of an ancient labour. The Knitting Map is not about knitting at all. It's about how to live. Listen.

Jools Gilson-Ellis and Richard Povall,
Artistic Directors,
The Knitting Map 2005

Preface

Voices of a European Capital of Culture

'There is a quiet chatter, banter, silence and the occasional comings and goings of people arriving and leaving their knitting stations, like genteel relay-runners. Before each of them, a digital screen details the next few lines of knitting and they press a foot pedal to advance the pattern. During the day, people arrive to view the installation. They hear low voices and the tapping of knitting needles. Before them this great knitted cartography, moves steadily along the floor of the crypt and begins to pile up in the half-light'. (half/ angel, 2005)

Maps never tell the real truth about a place. The reality of a place is always different. Maps have symbols – line spacings representing the lie of the land, perhaps the everydayness of a place – topography, water, road lengths, junctions, spot heights. In reality, those spacings are much different. In rural areas, colour can be seen, the horizon emerging in the distance, the changing seasons; in urban areas, one has hustle and bustle, people coming and going, discussion and laughter, traffic jams, colour, a living settlement created by human experience. Many places change with the numerous generations of people who inhabit, age and live out their lives within. The ideas of those generations adapt and transform. Ideals and morals alter, bringing revolutions in aspects such as fashion and architecture. New living landscapes are created, invoking new debate on culture.

Cork has developed by piecemeal transformation, a multi-layered and complex historical city, unique in that it developed originally on a series of marshy islands. It is the only Irish city that has experienced several phases of growth from an early Christian monastery to the Viking influence through the golden age of the Anglo-Norman walled town, the building of a new city centre in the eighteenth and nineteenth century to the urban renewal of today. The idea of Cork as a city has been and is being reinvented so much through the fulfilment of ideas of varied

St Patrick's Street in the Summer of 2005.

citizens, all striving to carve a niche for themselves in the life of the city. The varied surnames in Cork Street directories of yester-year are testament to the vision of those citizens making Cork home.

Cork has always been a cosmopolitan city within Western European culture, always staying in touch with aspects of modernisation. Its people and landscape have always been deeply linked with each other. Its development as a port especially being part of a wider empire in previous centuries, has helped city fathers to absorb ideas from those who had sailed to and explored the four corners of the world. Charles Smith, an antiquarian in 1750, recalled the multitude of ships docking in the City of Cork and the diverse accents chatting on the quays. Perhaps, if Cork was a person, its story would be richly embellished with tales of transformation and character.

The Knitting Map is an abstracted picture of how the city of Cork lived, breathed and went about its daily business throughout 2005. It is a beautiful and extraordinary object, extensive in scale and it tells the human story of the city. Looking at the stitch patterns up close, its craftsmanship is amazing. On more than one occasion attempting to photograph the Map close-up, I was left undecided on what to use in the book. On a workshop called the Pied Piper in late July 2005, when the map was carried through Cork's city centre, again its beauty could be seen as it was draped across the balustrade of Saint Patrick's Bridge.

It was a cold January evening in early 2005 when I first encountered Sue Tector Sands in the Cork Vision Centre. She enthusiastically described her involvement as Project Co-ordinator in a 2005 project called The Knitting Map. Immersed in curiosity, I attended the launch phase of the Map in the Cork 2005 House on Pope's Quay. I did not know what to expect. However, for those assembled, an adventure was just beginning; for others who had already been involved in the preliminary workshops, perhaps this was their special day. All were waiting for the off, like soldiers ready for battle or a revolution. One could not but admire their determination, belief and the warmth of their spirit for such a project. It was really inspiring, but as a historian-geographer, also intriguing to observe. The enthusiasm of the artistic directors Jools Gilson-Ellis and Richard Povall was infectious. The chat and banter could be heard in every room; in every corner, the culture of Cork, the problems of the world – the meaning of life – were all in a sense being discussed. That day, I became enchanted by the spell of the Map and chose to seize a new life opportunity; that day *Voices* was born, a publication to mark and perhaps map a cross-section of life experiences of those involved in The Knitting Map.

Voices aspires to widen the forum of discussion on all aspects of life in Cork in the year of European Capital of Culture 2005. Within this book, many of the stories reflect change, perhaps within the more emotional and spiritual landscape. *Voices* not only gives the Cork person a voice but also others from other parts of Ireland and wider parts of the world, who have been enchanted by The Knitting Map experience. It is very seldom in any city that such a broad community would come together and engage with each other on such a personal level. In fact, on several visits to the Map, I was met with people communicating with each other, who but only for the Map itself their life paths might never have crossed.

In *Voices*, the community of the Map (primarily women) have an opportunity to express their individual background, their memories, experiences, wonder, dreams and hopes. Like the assorted colours and patterns of The Knitting Map, the extremities of their life experiences are varied. Their creative energy is in essence woven together. Dispersed throughout the book are extraordinary stories of engaging and negotiating through the adventure of life. My earlier aims for this book have changed through meeting and getting to know the community of the Map. For me, what began as an oral history project has transformed into an artwork mapping life itself.

The community interviewed were allowed to find their own story through a series of leading questions but I was amazed that so many people chose to share their own personal life story without any questions asked! With every person interviewed, my imagination has been fired and on many occasions in the interview process, I was taken to other worlds. The titles of their story reflect their motto in life or their response on being asked what title they would give to their

The Lord Mayor of Cork visits with the knitters at the Project while the hard work continues in August 2005.

autobiography. Many of the stories in *Voices* have fallen (themselves) into four key sections: *The Knitting Map as a Revolution* – which charts the early origins of the Map and impressions of Knitting in society today. The section entitled *Growing Up and Family Life* maps several stories of growing up in Cork and gives impressions on how the city has changed physically, but also socially and culturally. The third section, *The Architecture of Life* explores what could be described as the pillars of modern society, from aspects such as marriage, death, divorce, disability and getting older and wiser (!) to the notion of womanhood. The fourth section entitled *Negotiating the Rhythms of Life* charts how several of The Knitting Map community have negotiated the later pillars of life, hence several of the stories explore tranquillity and finding oneself in the world.

Finally, one last note, it is perhaps very apt to have The Knitting Map, its craftsmanship and its associated traditions set in a church. Cork is a city of churches and has a skyline of spires. In exploring any church, one engages oneself with an age-old world tradition, religion, which is very much part of the human experience and is linked to community development. The construction of Saint

Luke's Church has been attributed to a number of factors. In the late eighteenth century, the building of Saint Patrick's Bridge in 1788 and the construction of new roads leading into the north-east quadrant of the then financially booming city, brought a new lease of life to the parish of Saint Anne's Shandon. On this basis, it was decided that a chapel-of-ease to Saint Anne's Church should be built. In 1837, the new chapel was consecrated by the Anglican Bishop of Cork, Samuel Kyle and dedicated to Saint Luke. The architects were Messrs. J. and George Richard Pain. This original chapel was an elaborate building of Gothic architecture of white limestone with two porches on either side of a narrow stylish spire.

In 1872, the profile of the surrounding area was raised when the parish of Saint Luke's was formed. This was located to the east of the Parish of Saint Anne's. Also, at this time, the running of the new parish church was taken over by a Rev. Mervyn Archdall, whose main priority was to construct a new church to cope with the growing population of the parish. Hence in January 1875, the second church was consecrated and opened to the public on the same site as the first. It was designed by Sir John Benson, who was also involved in the construction of Saint Patrick's Bridge in 1852. Twelve years after the initial opening, on the 9th February 1887, the church was completely gutted by fire and destroyed. A third church was rebuilt on the site and rededicated on the 8th February 1889. The edifice was designed by

The stained glass window in St Luke's Church in Summerhill showing the gathering of the community.

W.H. Hill and Thomas Anthony was the contractor, who was also responsible for the spire and entrance portico of Holy Trinity Church on Morrison's Island.

Saint Luke's Church highlights the rich tapestry of the history of its environs. It is a fascinating marker of the city's development through the ages and its diverse architectural style represents one of many phases in Cork's growth. The Church is a richly embellished with colour. The stained glass windows depict gatherings of communities. It highlights experiences from the Old and New Testament of the bible, elucidating such diverse themes as faith, hope, love and trauma. The voices of a different era echo throughout the building. In a sense, one is reminded of the community of The Knitting Map and their diverse backgrounds and life experiences.

The rich styled masonry of Saint Luke's Church, completed by local masons, is echoed in the blocks or stitches of The Knitting Map. Perhaps, the new masons are the community of The Knitting Map. What is clear is that Saint Luke's Church is now once again a space where old and new traditions collide, merge, diversify and, most importantly, are enjoyed by all.

Kieran McCarthy

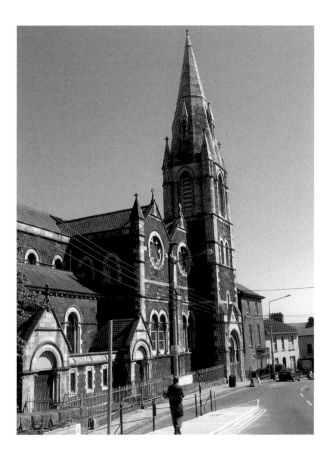

Chapter 1

The Knitting Map as a Revolution

'It's like you're making history but there's more to it than that – the whole underlying sociological perspective. It's the breaking down of boundaries on all sorts of different levels and bringing people out of the woodwork and re-connecting them'. (Kate O' Brien)

Kate O' Brien

How Do You Start a Revolution?

When I came to Cork, it was like a Florence, where everybody knows everybody and the city had the mentality of a village. The people are great – they let you into their lives. How did we find out where the knitters were? We went down to the wool shops where the source was and I hand wrote a note inviting people to sign up for a newsletter. Three hundred women signed up. A newsletter emerged through interviews. Knit-ins were arranged which were inspired by knit-ins in public places in England and America. It was the start of our revolution.

Public knit-ins were to be held on the last week of every month starting with the Crawford gallery – as the Map was an art project. We moved on to places like shopping centres, Shandon Craft Centre, trains, buses and anywhere where you wouldn't usually see women knitting. The sheer curiosity of it encouraged people to watch – kids in particular – guys laughed and joked but were still curious about the stitches noting: 'my mother used to do that!' So everyone began to notice that there was something happening in Cork, especially when Jools performed in costume in the middle of the street. People asked questions – is it street theatre? Is it the modeling of knit wear? Jools danced around like a warrior queen using needles as weapons. Before we knew it, we had hundreds of names on our databases for the newsletter, which was sent out every month.

At the first knit-in at the Crawford, we noticed the bonding beginning to happen. People began to talk about their knitting experience and then … anything. You must tell them a story of equal importance and that bonds you. The person on the other side of you joins in and all of a sudden you have a gang. In the Crawford, the first knit-in was amazing. That's a revolution – all over Cork and it gathered momentum. It became a huge party with deep friendships that you can't buy. it's like the French underground – all your lines overlap. The textile artists are like the generals. There is always someone on the ground.

We ended 2004 in the Women's Gaol Heritage Centre and it was quite remarkable. An old gaol by its nature has negative connotations. We thought it would be great to change the whole atmosphere of the gaol. We were like a group of revolutionaries and had a meeting – party – there… It was the worst day's weather but people came; I was in a cell but the door was open and I was knitting. The name of the women incarcerated were on the walls but yet, you were sitting there free – doing something that didn't feel like sitting very quietly in the corner knitting. I'm sitting here empowered. My knitting needles were weapons. The whole experience was militant.

The other great thing was the day of the Harley Davisons – a knit-in on bikes. I brought along spare helmets and a whole range of leathers for people to get in character to support the revolution. The biggest buzz was riding through the streets of Cork in rush hour traffic with no stops in the middle of thirty bikes. It's quite tribal.

It's like you're making history but there's more to it than that – the whole underlying sociological perspective. It's the breaking down of boundaries on all sorts of different levels and bringing people out of the woodwork and re-connecting them.

Mercy Foley

Labour of Love

My first adventure in knitting was when I was a child growing up in the early fifties in Barrett's Buildings on the northside of the city. We hadn't much but people had great loyalty to each other growing up. Northside people have great spirit and are very supportive. My family went to the Saint Vincent de Paul Sale of Work in Cork City Hall every Christmas. It would have lots of wool that would be knotted and given to them from Mahony's in Blarney. You could buy that wool very cheap and I remember my mother buying it. Our job as one of five daughters (and one brother) would be to get the wool out and take out the knots. I was taught to knit by my mother. I remember my mother buying lovely navy wool and knitting me a moss stitch jumper. I wore it to school and the nuns put me up on the table to show the craftsmanship of the jumper to my class. Many Cork companies would sell their products at the sale of work at City Hall at a reduced price. For example John Daly would sell Tanora which was practical for people at Christmas and it

came in small glass bottles. The wine and tea merchant on Academy Street, M.D. Daly, sold little packages of tea. There was a stall that gave raspberry or 'rasa' in bottles and you could keep it for Christmas and dilute it.

When I was a child, I used to go walking with my father, in Sunday's Well, through Fitzgerald's Park, out by the Lee baths and then out the Lee Road to pick blackberries. We would then come home and make blackberry jam. We'd play rounders, 'gobs' and skipping in the terrace where we lived. During the summer, if the weather was nice we were taken down to Youghal on the train. The night before, my brother and sisters and I would have our buckets and shovels ready. I think we had a very happy life growing up. I remember joining Sunday's Well Swimming Club and Councillor Gus Healy teaching me how to swim.

I have always enjoyed knitting and when the European Capital of Culture year started, I put my name down straight away. I was a tailoress by trade and served my time for five years with Jimmy Sorenson, a merchant tailor on the Lower Road. He made suits for such great people as Jack Lynch, Declan Dwyer, the Crosbies, Gerald Goldberg, gentry from the country, Theo O' Donovan – who I remember had a monocle in his eye – and Mr Jim Bell of Fota Island. I remember the button holes of the suits sewn with pure silk thread and the edges of the suit hand stitched. It was a great profession and I enjoyed it immensely. I then went to the Crawford Technical College and did a course two evenings a week, Monday and Thursday evenings. We did our London City and Guilds Certificate through that.

I remember as a student in the Crawford in 1955 and seeing the sky red-hot. We all ran down Washington Street and down to the Bridewell and looking down the quays and seeing the Opera House burning. It was a terrible tragedy. We had great memories of going especially at Christmas to the Panto. I remember queuing up on the steps at the side of the building up to the 'Gods'. Ignatius Comerford played the dame for many years. Gertie Wine was normally one of the main characters and was a beautiful singer. We might also go during the year. Jack Cruz might have a show on.

When I finished my course in the Crawford, I did a course on design in the College of Art in the late fifties. A job was advertised in the paper for Cork Polio in the textile department and I went for it and got the job. When I arrived first, we made aprons, tea cosies, towels, pillow cases baby gowns and curtains. I worked in Cope Foundation for nearly twenty years. It used to be Cork Polio when I started and I became a senior supervisor there as the years rolled on. John Birmingham founded Cope Foundation He was one of the first people to attempt to deal with polio in Cork. He started on the South Mall and eventually he built an organisation in Montenotte. Cope now have branches all over the County in Fermoy, Mallow, Macroom, Skibbereen, Kanturk and Mitchelstown. They have a very well established organisation, even worldwide now.

Some of my students are very good at music, knitting, sewing, drawing and painting. So I brought several of them to The Knitting Map every Monday. Women love coming up here to knit. It has been a great boost to them that they are involved in the project. I retired in May (2005). Cope had changed through the years. Supportive employment is a key part of the organisation now; getting clients to work in business and industry. On the continent, businesses are bound by law to provide a certain number of jobs to people with disability. Clients are very proud when they get their job. It is the start of something new. There is also a more diverse range of subjects to do, from art to knitting, drama and music.

I am enjoying my retirement immensely. I wake up in the morning and think what will I do today. I am not a bit bored with my retirement. I have four grown up children, two boys and two girls. I am a grandmother and have three granddaughters. My husband, who was a cooper with Irish distillers, is also retired. He was one of the last coopers to serve his time in Cork. None of my family turned to craft. Perhaps it is too slow in today's world. I feel that idle hands are no good for anybody. I do feel that children today spend too much time with Playstations and that there should be a lot more story sessions in school. Children should be encouraged to love nature classes, learning about life, animals and plants.

Betty Flynn

Beyond Vision

Everybody at some stage has thought about writing their life story and consequently, I'm no different. I thought about writing mine a long time ago. I grew up in the Blackwater Valley, three miles from Mallow in the townland of Lacknamona. I was an only child and so I had to rely a lot on my own devices to keep myself amused. My parents split up when I was child and so I didn't grow up with either of them around. It was my grandparents that reared me and were my influences growing up. My grandfather was a very craft orientated person. He did not do anything else other than agricultural work and I learnt a lot from him.

I had a problem with my eyesight – I was born with *congenital achromotopsia*. I am sensitive to the light and have no colour vision. I see everything in black and white. It can be awful at times as colour is everywhere. People talk about it and describe it in detail. I hid the problem for a long time and then came clean eventually. Imagine a world without colour; imagine depending on the light for how much you can see; bumping blindly into things in bright sunlight – yet also the joy of going for a walk at dusk on a May evening.

As a child, growing up in the fifties, I attended a small country school where, using four-ply wool and number twelve needles, we had to learn to knit. The

theory was easy enough but I found it almost impossible to master this practice and the teacher dismissed me rather impatiently. I could not physically see the wool. My uncle spotted where I was going wrong, took me aside and with a ball of twine and two pieces of sticks, he showed me what to do. I never looked back. This kindly act opened up a whole new world of possibilities. I slowly mastered the art, spurred on by visions of dolls' jumpers and any other creation that could be knit. Before long, I was making my own cardigans. Being an avid reader, it was an exhilarating experience learning to follow a knitting pattern.

I left school when I was fifteen as it was tough going. I had completed a year at second level in Mallow. I went to work for a local farmer for the remainder of teenage years. In the sixties, I then went to work as a shop assistant for the company Liptons in the sixties, who then had several branches in County Cork. I got married and made the choice to devote most of my time to rearing a family. I had four children, three of which are surviving. I have one grandchild and one on the way. With knitting, I could physically do something, especially being a young mother stuck at home with the kids. I made their clothes. I got great satisfaction out of something you made and which cost a quarter of what you would buy it for.

The early sixties saw a huge revival of the Aran sweater due to the popularity in Ireland of a folk group known as the Clancy Brothers. This band of singer /songwriters wore their hand-knitted traditional jumpers all over the world with pride and started a new upmarket fashion trend. My most prized possession at the time was an Aran dress, which took hours of concentration to complete. Wool was very inexpensive in those days and the system of personal service in wool stores was ideal for me because I was ashamed of being colour blind and would not admit to it. In due course, I found a mail order catalogue, which served my purpose for many years. My confidence in completing the difficult stitch structures of Aran knitting grew and I began to knit professionally for various companies around the country. As my family got older, I thanked God that none of them had inherited my eye condition and there was no longer a shadow hanging over their creativity. One of my greatest wishes was fulfilled when my daughter, Mel, became a professional knitwear designer.

Towards the early nineties, I was forced to stop knitting as my eyes were troublesome and it was only then that I sought a second opinion. I was introduced to a self-help programme called the *Island of the Colour Blind*, which explained everything in full. No longer feeling the need to hide my problem, I registered with The National Council for the Blind and learned of their fantastic craft classes. I have been a member ever since and their help has changed my life.

The Knitting Map has great design and imagination. We have put Cork on the map with needles! Every Monday, a group of eight to ten women, all with vision impairments, come together for a morning of knitting and friendship. Their bonds are very strong because it all began back in 1991. Catherine Lowney suggested the idea to another long-time National Council of the Blind member Nóirín O' Flynn. In recent years, the Sisters of Mercy offered the ground floor room at the Saint Mary's of the Isle Convent on Sharman Crawford Street to a constantly expanding number of skilled knitters. The knitting classes acquired the help of teacher. Maureen McGrath in 1993 and since then, regular garments have been sent to Bosnia and Romania. I am simply a relatively new recruit in their midst.

In recent months, the members of the class have designed and made colourful rugs and shawls for distribution to the house bound and elderly blind in the area. The social aspect and the knowledge that these skills contribute are important – the fact that the end product is aesthetically beautiful but practical makes all the commitment and hard work worthwhile for everyone. President Mary McAleese has one of these designer rugs, courtesy of Cork Tape Magazine presenter, Joan Murphy, a long-time supporter of the group. The last box of knitting was approximately one square metre in size and went to the Chernobyl Children's Project, with another almost completed. They are a selfless band of volunteers who have been the backbone behind a vast selection of charitable projects. They show to the world how they can see beyond boundaries, whether physical, cultural or geographical, which opens up a whole new realm of opportunity with limitless perspective. They single-handedly expanded my horizon and the future's so bright – I'm wearing shades.

Caroline Kearney

I like Knitting

I like knitting, crochet and patchwork – you can make lots of things. I started knitting on the Map last year and I enjoy meeting the people involved with the Map and the people that come and visit it. I was born in London but was raised in Ballyphehane. My favourite memory was going to school and I went to two schools. I went to a school in Mayfield with my sister and in the afternoon, I went to Queen of the Angels in Montenotte. I now work in Q.D.S in Togher and do a lot of craftwork there. Cork is a nice place. I like going to town, going out to restaurants and going out to the Country Club on a Saturday night.

Marion O' Sullivan

People Can Talk... Make Friends... Learn to knit

My life has changed a lot especially since my divorce. There are always downs in life. So make sure you enjoy it. Seven years ago, I met a man who I look up to. This man has given me confidence and encouraged me to go out – that you can do anything. He realises that I have been knitting and have loved it since my school days. I am knitting or doing crochet every night. He has noticed a positive change in me since I got involved in The Knitting Map. It has never come between us – he said it is 'my thing'.

Last year, I got involved into the workshops of The Knitting Map. The people are fabulous. Knitting has come back in such a big way with this project this year and last year. Knitting was on the way out. With a ball of wool, you can knit anything – a hat, a doll. I am always knitting at home. I remember one year I made twelve dolls in twelve months, Santa Claus, clowns, a ballerina, a pirate. It was a great stress release from the problems in my marriage. For people associated with the Map, they have made friends. They meet up afterwards and they may go to see a show or go somewhere together. For me personally, I have met great people and am impressed to hear what they have achieved. You have from the young knitter up to the old knitter. People can talk; have a cup of tea and a scone. They have made friends and things have moved on from there.

Ena Atkinson

Knitting is History. It Has Been Around a Long Time

My first visit to Cork was fifty years ago on my honeymoon. I remember the River Lee, ringing the Shandon Bells and we stayed with my husband's (Johnny) sister on the Wellington Road. My husband had a Ford Prefect, a year or two old. We also went to Kenmare, to a little church called Saint John's in Glengarrif and to Garnish Island. We went down there yesterday to see if we would remember anything… it was all very different.

I am from near Ardattin near Tullagh, Co. Carlow. I was brought up in Co. Wexford, near Kilrush. I was raised on a farm, helped with everything from milking the cows to thrashing. I had one brother and sister. We had no television. We had good fun on the farm, laughing and joking with the workmen, all innocent fun. We had records and listened to them on the gramophone. We learned to dance to the records, the cuckoo waltz on the flag floor of the farm house. I went to a boarding school in Wexford, which many farmers' daughters went to. Before I finished my education, my mother became sick and I had to stay at home to mind her. That finished me thinking of nursing or any other profession.

My mother always knitted and sewed and I learnt from her. It is relaxing, something to do with your hands. In my local Irish Country Women's Association, we helped revive the Borris lace, a tape lace with needle and fine thread from Co. Carlow. It was successful but it was a slow and difficult technique. We thought it

was necessary to keep the old crafts going. We entered some pieces in the Royal Dublin Society (R.D.S.) and received several awards. It was a sign that it was recognised. I also like old embroidery. If you think about it, in the past, women would lace make by candle light or sunlight – a great feat of craftsmanship.

I got married early in life. I have five children, the youngest is forty and the oldest is fifty. I have fourteen grandchildren and I feel they are going on a different path of life. Morals are very different now to our day. To be good is more difficult today. I get on well with my grandchildren. They come and go when they can. My grand-daughter who is seven chose to stay with me at the weekend instead of going off with her mam and brother to a pony event in Tralee. I felt it was an honour for me that she chose to stay.

Sr Kathleen Hopkins

It's a Gift for the Area

I came to Cork in 1995 and I started a club in 61 Roches Buildings. It was called Sr Kathleen's Wednesday Afternoon Club. I started and wanted to keep it as a craft club. I started with eight members and now have 28 members... In the club, I run a Christmas and summer fund, so people can have a little extra. It is the purpose of saving for holiday time, which is severe on the pocket, which is important. We have a sale of work in November to raise money for charity. We keep it a small

Sr Kathleen's Wednesday Afternoon Club in July 2005.

venture, as we wouldn't be able to cope with crowds coming. We have a raffle and out of that money or donations we get, we save for our big outing in June every year. This year, we went to Millstreet Country Park, Saint John's Holy Well and had our dinner in Killarney. The thought of being together makes the day so enjoyable. Togetherness makes it whole and the aims of the club are fulfilled – to know one another and to know someone in need, to help them, to give them the kind word. The ideas for the club come from being on life's road and you develop them as you go and as the years roll on.

The ladies in my club meet once a week or we could meet in town. We could have a cup of tea and a chat. There is something to that and I hope that the ladies are getting as much out of the club as I am. We have knitted vests for those children from poorer backgrounds in the maternity wards in the city and sent clothing to Belarus. I saw The Knitting Map on the paper a year ago. I was interested that the ladies got involved. The Project is a gift to the area.

On an outing, I'm really thrilled that the ladies in the club bond so well together. They are kind and watch out for one another. It's amazing that on outings we all try to give each other space but eventually we all end up in the same hotel for our dinner or tea. We went one year to Dublin to Harold's Cross Heritage Centre. I asked should we book a carriage. They said they would scatter through the train. Every one of us ended up in the one carriage. We played cards and joked all the way to Dublin.

Teresa Geary

We had Good Times and Bad Times

Going to Dublin was a culture shock. I was originally from Galway and I moved to Dublin to get a job in nursing. It was the first time I was on a train. We ate breakfast – cereal and tea and toast. It was always brown bread and eggs at home. I remember eating 'cheerios' for the first time! I had come from a place where everything was slow. The city outlook is a different way of life to being raised on a farm with your own supplies of food. In the city, everything has to be brought in. City people take for granted how food stuffs come about. Country people are different to city people. In fact, Dublin people will talk to you but they are slightly detached. Cork people are much warmer. They will make you feel that they are talking to you. I met my husband in Dublin who was a Corkman.

I began training to be a nurse in Dublin in the late forties. I didn't carry it through because in those days when you married, you had to leave the workplace. I think that it was not until the 1970s that women could hold a job in the civil service if they got married. The thinking was that it was a waste of time educating women because they would get married anyway. Women were seen as good house-keepers. As the years went by, I regret not becoming a nurse – I could have gone back to work.

Knitting was my passion for years. In the west of Ireland, women were judged by their creative ability. Women transformed the ten stone Odlum's flour bag into

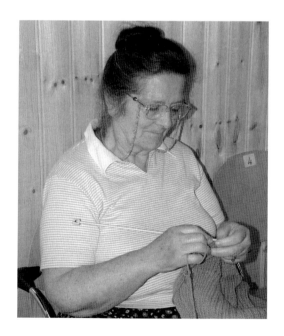

shirts, tea cloths and tea cosies. Women were even judged if they could not remove or bleach out the brand name Odlum's. My teacher used to knit and taught my class. It took me a while to learn the knitting techniques. My teacher had ten in her family and she was always knitting socks. I was always fascinated how you could get plain on one side and pearl on the other. I got four match sticks and twine and discovered how to do the stitches. When I had my children, I knitted a garment once a week. I made all their clothes. Knitting was entertainment and satisfaction. At one time, when my marriage broke up, I had nothing to live on. I knitted for a year. I barely got by and got a good job as a cook in a farmhouse. The job was time-consuming and I had to give up the knitting.

For the past twenty years, I have lived in a cottage near Mallow next to my eldest son. I live alone. I have a son in Australia, one in Cornwall, one in California and a daughter in New York. I live from day to day and plan holidays with my friends. I also belong to the Traditional Irish Lace Makers for the past eight years. I spend a lot of time making lace. We meet once a month and go away for weekends. Motto in life? Don't feed it and it won't grow. That's what I tell my grown up children when they have a problem and are going on about it.

Maureen McGrath

A Knitting Education

I feel The Knitting Map is great for people to get together. It's a work of art that puzzles me. It looks like someone looking out of a plane looking down at fields. All my life I've been knitting, I find it relaxing. Knitting provides pleasure and therapy for me. I remember I started knitting when I was eight years old. It was at Glountaune National school and I used to go to my teacher's house after tea and she used to teach me. Mrs Shaw was her name. We also used to do tapestry, crochet and needlework.

Sr Mary Ryan

Make the most out of life

My mother was very involved in crafts, knitting and crochet. That's how I started knitting. When I was nursing, I did the odd bit of knitting. I did a knitting course with Mary McGregor in Sunday's Well and I entered some garments for the Cork Summer Show. I got first prize in one of the categories. I love knitting. It is relaxing and I get great satisfaction out of it. The more difficult the pattern is the better. My motto in life is to make the most of it while I can.

Maureen McGrath

Sr Mary Ryan

Mel Murphy

Life is Too Short to Drink Bad Coffee

The Knitting Map is a work of art, a record of the stitches that will have huge historical value in years to come. I think people knit because the knitter can have something to be proud of. It is a unique artwork that you can do for someone else. I would be frightened to think of my kids growing up and not knowing how to knit or sew, how to make things and not knowing the value of creativity. Knitting is a skill that could be extinct very easily. It just needs a generation not to know how to knit.

I remember when I was younger my mum made me a cardigan and an outfit to match. I remember I wore it going to school. I was just eight or nine. The teacher made me walk up to the top of the class and made me do a twirl. The design was so unusual and beautiful. I am originally from CastletownRoche in North Cork and I was thought how to knit in school. My mother used to knit Aran sweaters for Blarney Woollen Mills. I learned to do more difficult patterns by watching her. It was easier than reading the patterns. With knitting you really have to be shown how to do it.

I did social studies in College and was working with kids in a crèche. The kids used to come in and show me their designer clothes. I always knew I wanted to do something more creative. I decided to do fashion design in the College of Commerce. I kept my job going for a year. After two years, I then did a course a hand knitting design course, a City and Guilds Course. I was more interested in the craft more than the machine side of those courses. I was brought up at home with that interest.

When I finished my studies, I was still uncertain what to do. I knew I wanted to explore knitwear and the angle I wanted to develop was kids-wear. I had experience

in knowing what made kids tick. I began making clothes for kids and set up my own design label called 'Alterknitive Design'. If you make something unusual for a child, you can make something that people will interact with; they will interact with the child. My clothes are geared towards craft shops. While I was in college, we were given names of various state and regional bodies to contact if we ever were to set up our own business. I always wanted to work for myself. I had a personal drive and it was the South Cork Enterprise Board that helped put me on the road. They provided me with funding and gave me a mentor who also had an interest in textiles as well.

With any business though, there are trials and tribulations. Trying to maintain a business is always very tough. It's a roller coaster ride and you must go with the business. You never know what's going to happen next. You're dealing with so many variables. When you're creating something, you're very stuck in it. It's very hard to detach yourself from the product. It actually becomes your baby. What makes it worthwhile for me is when someone comes back in and says they bought clothes from me and that the child loved it. I now have to take time out due to my pregnancy – another roller coaster ride, my emotions are all over the place. You go from nervousness to panic to joy… I can't wait to see what the baby will look like.

Grace Madden

Enjoying the Map

I am from the Glen. I didn't like growing up there. It was rough and some people were bad. I now live in Montenotte. I like The Knitting Map project. I only started knitting only a couple of months ago… I really enjoy it.

Enrika Bertolini Cullen

The Diamond in the Rough

I arrived in Ireland on a grey cold November evening in 1969 to take up a position in Inishfree Pottery in Sligo Town. It was my first trip by plane, my first 'real' job and I had no English as I studied French at School. At 21 years of age, it was an adventure and 35 years later, I feel it still is. I married an Irish man with a transferable job. We moved house regularly going back sometime to a different part of the same county. Galway, Sligo, Cavan, Monaghan, Offaly and Kildare are my home territories where friends and neighbours are located who I have kept in touch with over the years. For a long time, I was a home mum to four children – two boys and two girls and my art interests and teaching career were put on hold to give space to their upbringing. I knew that once the family grew up, I would have time and space to go back to previous interests. I am still after all Italian and very attached to my roots and my upbringing, even if my Italian brogue is a little more refined now!

The coptic circle as designed by Enrika Bertolini Cullen.

I was born and grew up in a town in Northern Italy, Reggio Emilia, known mainly for giving birth to the Italian tricolour flag and of this I am very proud. Since my early childhood, I had two great loves, animals and art. I attended the local Art College and furthered my education for three years at the International School of Pottery in Faenza. It is now I fully appreciate that thanks to the dedication and commitment of my tutors, I received a very broad and versatile education and that those formative years paved the way to approaching different projects with a little trepidation but nonetheless enthusiasm. This approach can also be said to be true of The Knitting Map.

My involvement with the Map was due to the need to create a space that provided both a suitable home to the knitters and a display area for the artwork as it grew. I felt The Knitting Map could only be presented as a cascading and rippling continuity to maximise the visual impact of such a spectrum of colours and variety of texture. So a certain light was needed. In order not to interfere with the art piece created, the technology needed to be discretely incorporated into the installation and the material used for the construction of it had to be natural and unobtrusive. The coptic circle, in spite of its scale, was intended to leave that sense of intimacy that is associated with a group knitting. I grew up in a household where knitting, embroidery, sewing, crochet were a group event. It was a daily occurrence to hear the clicking of wooden needles and the chattering of women sitting in the garden in a circle and between holding up hanks and winding balls of wool. Instinctively then, the semicircular shape came to mind. After designing the installation, I assisted Seanny Berett – the young craftsman who made and put together the pieces of this elaborate jigsaw – in an advisory capacity. I was very pleased with the results and the space allocated to it in the crypt of Saint Luke's Church. It is in a way a home from home as the venue with the Church of Ireland building and I have made my home in Saint Columba's Church, Tullamore, which also was a Church of Ireland building. Life is full of coincidences.

Much hard work has gone into the conversion – money and a serious amount of research – as I firmly believe that any job you do the best you can and you can only do it once. I often refer to my home as 'my diamond in the rough'. Very few people apart from my family realise what rough means at times. Like all diamonds, I am almost at the polishing stage and in a way not before its time, but now here in Durrow, I have combined my original two loves – animals and art – and with my children's age going from thirty to twenty-four, much of my time is now my own. The stained glass windows, the arches, altar area, old tiled floors, which so carefully were retained as 'important feature', create an inspiring atmosphere. I have several small groups of girls for classes. To all of them, two hours of painting is an opportunity to take time out from daily pressures and share worries and achievements. I regularly visit the the nearby Durrow monastery, where the scribe of the illuminated manuscript of the *Book of Durrow* and the High Cross once lived. Is it a coincidence that for many years, long before I came to Offaly, a lot of my work has Celtic influences? I am sure that in spite of all the physical work, the rubble, the dust, the financial restraints, the researching, the pleading with the workmen, at the end of the day this will be the most important of my art work; the most elaborate of my installations and I am privileged to live in it.

Chapter 2

Growing Up and Family Life

'When I think about it, I have really good memories but of nothing spectacular and I wonder about the kids that have the computers and the holidays in Spain and they have their bikes – will they have good childhood memories when they grow up?'(Ann Ralph)

Ann Ralph

I Promise to be as Good as Gold

I was thinking about my childhood as far as holidays were concerned. When I was a child, you didn't go to Spain or France. We thought it was the best thing going that we went down to Youghal. My dad worked in C.I.E. and we'd go down to Youghal during the week. You'd practically have a carriage to yourself. I always loved the train. The only thing I remember about Youghal is that we used to go up on the hill at the end of the strand. There was a woman up there that used to sell pots of boiling water for six pence. My mother had brought the tea leaves and the milk and soggy tomato sandwiches and biscuits. It's one of the clearest memories I have of my childhood.

During the summer, the older girls in our terrace in Farranree used to take us to Fitzgerald's Park. We used to walk over and going across the Shaky Bridge – someone would always jump. So, we'd all be screaming and roaring and tearing across to get to the park. We spent hours sitting whilst having a picnic of a bottle of diluted orange and marietta biscuits. We always had to have someone older to take us out there. You'd always have to go begging and borrowing and promising to be as good as gold but sure God love us, we never were. If it wasn't there, it was down the pond by what is now the Common's Inn. We used to catch tadpoles there and bring them home and put them in the bath, but sure the poor things would be dead within hours. When I think of it my mother put up with a lot – practically every time we went down there we brought tadpoles and they all died.

When I think about it, I have really good memories but of nothing spectacular and I wonder about the kids that have the computers and the holidays in Spain and they have their bikes – will they have good childhood memories when they grow up? When I was growing up no one went on foreign holidays, many Cork people would go to Robert's Cove or Crosshaven. They would have a caravan there or their family might have a caravan down there. Some families would move down there for the summer. Our summer was the green and it was entertaining yourself basically – playing football and playing pickey. I don't know if kids today know what pickey is. It is a proper Irish version of Hopscotch. I never won at pickey. I obviously have no co-ordination. Breda Fitzgerald who lived two doors down always won – no matter what, I could never get it.

I used to go over to my grandmother who used to live on the Old Blackrock Road. My grandfather was a watchman in the Cork Gas Works. My grandparent's house had no electricity, no running water and an outside toilet. I used to love going down to her. She used to always bake. It might be only brown bread or a currant loaf. She never had a recipe – it was a case of a handful of this and a cup of this and mix it all up and bang it in the gas oven with the one gas light.

It used to be a treat to stay with my grandmother during the summer. I stayed there with my older sister, well one week each. I remember clearly lighting the oil lamp. My grandmother died in 1968 and there was no running water. She used to catch rainwater in a barrel outside. She always said it was great to watch your hair in rainwater. She always brushed out her long grey hair at night before she went to bed. That was a lovely house; it was old, cosy and small. She used to have a great fireplace with a settle, a seat covered with leather and we used to sit by the fire. We used to love to play with the bellows. She was a lovely woman. My uncle had created a small flower bed and she had aubretia hanging down over it all the summer with loads of blue flowers. Around the corner nearby to where the toilet was located (which was a bucket in a shed) was the vegetable garden… it was such a beautiful garden.

Sally Buckley

It was a very simple time but we were very happy

Our world was Blackrock and the month we spent in Crosshaven every summer. I have one brother and one sister and I am the oldest. When we were very young in the 1950s, we lived in Barrington's Avenue in Ballintemple in a one-storey house. I actually remember when I was four, following my cousin down to school and the little nun that was teaching us was Mother Evangela. In 1960, we moved to a two storey house on Church Road. In 1964, I moved with my husband to Montenotte.

I remember we entertained ourselves. We played as children in Blackrock which was the country with plenty fields and very little housing, very different to today. I always remember on a Sunday, many people from the city used to come down to Blackrock Castle and have their picnic. We used to say that 'the "townies" are down here again'. There was one lady who would sell oranges and apples at a stall at the Castle and everyone would buy her wares. We went swimming where the Lee Tunnel now is. Our picnics as children consisted of bottles of water and bread and jam. That area of Ballinure and Ballinure Cottages are all housing estates now.

Another great past-time was catching bees in jam jars with holes in the lid. We used to skip and we had different rhymes to switch people. *'I don't know who it is – I got a shock of nerves and I called my Mary in'*…and that person would jump in with you, *'Mary light the candle Mary light the gas, run in, run out, there's someone under the bed'*… then another person would run. We'd play pickey by chalk drawing boxes with numbers in them on the footpath. We threw a tennis ball up against the wall, the rhyme went: *'Billy Baker, biscuit-maker had a wife and couldn't keep her, had a mother, he couldn't love her, up the chimney he did shove her, what do you think he had for supper? Two boiled eggs and poisoned butter'.*

The games we played at home were shop and house. We had no toys and we had no television just a radio. We had to use our imagination. On a rainy day in my mother's dining room, my sister, my brother and I would create a house out of a table and even put up curtains. One of the boys would be the husband. I used to be the wife and use the name Mrs. O' Callaghan…I just liked the name. We'd use the dining room chairs as the bus. We used to recreate Mass and the Communions with a polo-mint. My brother was the priest and the same sermon was given every time – about Saint Patrick and his call. On a wet day, that's what you'd do. It was a very simple time but we were very happy.

As we got older in our early teens, my friends and I went to dances in Saint Columba's Hall in Douglas. It's still there. We used to cycle there. I remember the bands, Christy Daniels and Robbie Kearney .We had to be home by half past ten or eleven or end up in a lot of trouble. The Well Road and Skehard Road were house free and just narrow byroads. We were one of the lucky people. We got a holiday in a bungalow in Crosshaven every summer for a month. My mother saved for a year and she was a great manager. It was the highlight of the year.

Blackrock was made up of various people, the village people, the comfortable, the richer people in the big houses on the Castle Road. Fishing was the big thing in Blackrock Castle… but we all went to one school, the Ursuline Convent. Many people in Blackrock were related in some way.

Rose Conlon

Be Optimistic, Not Pessimistic

I learned to knit and sew from a very early age (in the 1940s-1950s) from my mother and in my school, the North Presentation Convent. I remember the nuns in school setting up a competition between classes to make a dress or petticoat. I got first prize and it gave me a great outlet all my life. I enjoyed school and was a quick learner but I was a bit of a rebel and a tomboy. I left at Inter Cert level and began a long career in clothes making. I started making items first by hand and then when I was seventeen my mother bought me a hand machine. I made my own clothes and those of my children. I also made clothes for other people. I made all my daughters wedding dresses. Knitting has changed my life.

At seventeen, I went to work with the clothing factory Dwyers on Washington Street. I was there for two years and then I was laid off and went to work for Cohens on Winthrop Avenue. Maurice Cohen was great to work for and we made boys and men's suiting. Shortly afterwards, they moved to Saint Augustine's Street. In 1960, at the age of 21, I moved to England with my boyfriend, John, a Corkman, who had been working in London for several years. The pace was

Walking on 'Pana', me on right

Me with friends and family in
Fitzgeralds Park

much faster in London than it was in Cork. We worked on conveyor belts and everybody was paid on piece work. We stayed there for over a year and came home for my sister's wedding in Cork. In the winter of that year 1961, I married John in Ballyphehane Church.

I was born in the North Mall and raised on Batchelor's Quay. When I was growing up, the area was a quiet one. There were very few children to play with. It was the opposite when I moved to my grandmother's house on Batchelor's Quay. My grandfather was Daniel Gamble, a city councillor and he campaigned successfully to get free milk for the poor. My father also expressed an interest in politics. I remember also that my father and uncle loved music and they knew all the arias from the operas and operettas and they'd be harmonising. When I was in school, we sung the opera *Mauritania* with the boys from the North Monastery. We had some beautiful singers in our class – Noelle Callanan was one. She sung in the Belle of New York weeks before the Opera House was burned down in 1955. I still sing today in the church choir in Ballyphehane Church.

We lived in one of the big Georgian Houses on Bachelor's Quay and in time the block of houses was condemned to be demolished. At that stage, my grandmother had already moved to Douglas to look after her sister's family who had died. Our family were to be re-housed in Ballyphehane. I was seventeen and it was a major change to move. When I moved there first, the bus only came to the start of the Kinsale Road and we had to walk the full length of Pearse Road to get home. The Togher bus came as far the Lough. In those days, the roads were very quiet with very little traffic and very safe to cycle. The new house was equipped with modern conveniences – a bathroom and running hot water; on Batchelor's Quay, there was just an outdoor toilet. Some of my neighbours on the Quay were moved to other areas in the city such as Spangle Hill (Farranree). The community was broken up. Some of the girls I grew up with, I didn't see them again for years. I kept in contact with my best friend, Margaret, who lived on Grattan Street and we married into the same family – marrying two brothers.

Jane Duggan

A True Corkonian!

I can go back six generations. We never had a country relative. Our family, Gamble, were city through and true and were very well known in the 'marsh'. I suppose that makes me a true Corkonian. I was named after my grandmother. My father had two brothers and the eldest of their families was called Jane. I am Rose Conlon's sister who also knits on the Map. Our stories are linked but different in a sense that she was more an outdoor person while I was always at home. We had different interests. I was the eldest in my family and I spent a lot of time with my father who was involved in politics. My grandfather, Danny Gamble was an alderman with the Labour Party. He was known to be a champion of the poor and their rights. He was very conscious of the poorer citizens and many a time he inspected and commented on the soup at the Cork Union Workhouse, now Saint Finbarr's Hospital. He had a sheet metal factory on Grattan Street. My father, Eddie, worked in Fords but when business got slack in the forties, he and his brother carried on their father's business in sheet metal.

I was very close to my father and spent time with him after school down in his workshop on Grattan Street. I used to go with him to political rallies on Sunday morning. I remember sitting on a platform with Eamonn DeValera standing on it in Blackrock. I still have an interest in current affairs. Theatre and music are also great loves of mine. My father and mother were part of the Fr. Mathew Hall Players and great singers. I can remember every Monday night when I was very young going to the Opera House to see ballet, Shakespearean companies, Carl Rosa Opera Company and the Carl Clopet Company. I always loved knitting. My mother was a great knitter and crochet worker and she taught me those skills from the age of five.

I was a secretary in James Brennan Wholesale Company in Tuckey Street. They imported raw cork wood from Portugal in Spain and used to cut the corks for the breweries, Beamish and Murphys. They also imported china and earthenware from England and were the main suppliers to hotels such as the Imperial and the Metropole.

Cork is a great city. It has a lot going for it. The infrastructure is good, plenty of refurbishment and employment. The working class people of the past are now able to send their children to university. What has not changed though are the cliques of people. Inequality within the social system in Cork and Ireland needs to be watched. There are not half enough watch-dogs; people not paying taxes and making money... My life motto? Do the best I can for people. I always try to help, do a good turn. I count myself lucky every day, for my husband, my daughters and my grandchildren. That is my success in life. I am happy to see my children doing well in life.

Mary O' Driscoll & Teresa Hallahan (sisters, née Cummins)

Blackrock: A Fishing Story

We're true Rockies and still follow the hurling in Blackrock... I was born in 1929 (Mary) and I come from a family of thirteen. We lived in a small house, a kitchen, another room, two bedrooms and a loft. My sister Teresa still lives on the spot. We had a big yard and used to grow cabbage there. We had no running water. When we were young, the younger children were put in a hammock made from fishing nets. We were poor enough but my mother managed. Nine of us have survived.

My father used to make and mend the nets in Blackrock. My mother and my family used to help wind the twine around house chairs in such a way that a mesh net could be created. My father used to go fishing and we'd eat fish, in particular salmon – it has put me off eating fish today. In those days, the fish caught were brought up by boat to the market where they were sold. In later years they were brought by bus, the stink from them did not go down too well. My father used

to make the boats from start to finish, 26 ft. boats in our yard over the winter months. The season opened on the 1st February and you had to get a licence to fish, which cost five shillings. They used to make the nets in the house, a sort of knitting. They had lines hanging on the quay walls to dry the nets.

We played on the green by the piers in Blackrock and swam in the front and at the back of Blackrock Castle. We were always skipping and we'd use the long ropes my father had for the boats. There would be three or four of use skipping at the same time. We also played 'tops and whips'. My father used to make the spinning tops and you would use a string to whip them around.

I remember the boating regattas on the Marina and each side of the event was black with people. There was a swimming baths at Brighton House. The area was called the Baths Strand and every morning before school, we'd gather driftwood and cork for our fire. The city trams used to go to the end of Blackrock. I also remember my brothers making their confirmation together, one nine, ten and the other eleven. They were on the altar together. It was the eldest brother that earned the money to buy suits, ten pounds each.

Blackrock has changed a lot in recent years, much more housing – it was all water and fields before. We knew everyone from Blackrock village to the next village at Ballinure. It's all strangers now. When we were young, we'd walk to the market gardens of Ballinure and pick potatoes and cabbage. I remember cycling to the farmers of lakelands, now built on by Jacob's Island, to get milk.

Dolores Cummins

Cork: Capital of Activity

I remember visiting my aunts at the age of four or five in Blackrock Village (1960s). I went to school for a time in the Ursuline Convent. Then my parents moved to town. My father died when I was young and there were eight of us. So my father's family remained close. We lived in Tower Street near to town, it was safe and everyone knew each other. I went to South Presentation Convent, Primary and Secondary Schools. I see it's set to close next year. It was an all-girl's school and they had beautiful gardens there. I loved it. There were 36 in my class and there were five hundred students attending the schools.

I remember going to Eglantine baths; there was one pool for the boys and one for the girls. We went to Douglas Baths and Fitzgerald's Park. Every Sunday, we would go to Blackrock to visit our relations. We used to go dancing at the downtown campus, the Arcadia. Rock bands used to play there. U2 and UB 40 started off there. We didn't go to pubs before we went dancing. We never drank as I was involved in the Fr. Mathew clubs. Members of the Club were one of the first

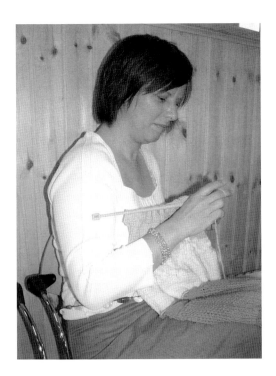

non-basketball teams to play basketball in official leagues. We won the league and the championship in the late seventies.

Liam McCarthy

A King's Lifestyle on a Pauper's Budget

I was born in Chapel Hill, four doors from the North Cathedral. My parents rented a small room in the front of a small house. They already had a daughter even though Ma was only 21. After my brother was born, we moved to Church Avenue to a small two-up-two-down house where there were eventually nine of us living.

The eldest of us grew up during the war, so times were extremely hard on my parents trying to make ends meet. There was a great community spirit with neighbour helping neighbour, because food was rationed people often ran short so they would borrow a pinch of tea, a sup of milk and so on from each other. Gas was also rationed and turned on for a limited time morning, noon and evening. To heat water for washing or bathing kids they used a sawdust fire which smouldered all day long and took hours to boil a kettle. The bath was a galvanised tub hanging on a nail in the yard. We had a tap in the yard and an outside toilet. As there was little construction during the war and as my father was a plasterer, he was idle for

long periods of time. He would get up in the morning around 6 a.m. and after a cup of tea and a bit of bread he would walk to the five builders yards, calling to them in rotation on a day-by-day basis to see if they had work. If he was refused, he would go to the labour-exchange and sign for the dole, he would then walk to Woodford-Bournes corner and stand there all day. If a builder needed a man he would select one from those waiting, the other trades stood at Barry's corner and the National Monument, etc.

To supplement our income, Ma paid a handyman to knock a hole in the wall between the front room and the narrow hall, put in a shelf counter, put a shelf in the window, sold the furniture in the room, got credit from Cliffords in Shandon Street and started a grocery shop. She also became an agent for YP pools of Liverpool – a forerunner of the lotto. Myself and my siblings sold the pools in the neighbourhood – 'you forecast the scores in the English football matches' – my siblings were good at sales, but I was useless. The corporation gave us a small plot in Fair Hill, the loan of a pike and fork and seed potatoes etc. so we could grow our own food. The parents then were fantastic to put up with the hardship.

On the other side of the coin, the neighbourhood was always ready for a hooley. Any excuse for a singsong or a dance and Tim Lordon, 'God be good to him', would bring out the gadget and a chair and they would sing and dance into the small hours. If a neighbour was sick or hard-up, there was always comfort and help available.

As kids the lifestyle to us was normal and the Northside was a kid's paradise. We spent our time playing hurling, football and handball. We swam in the Lee at the Lee Fields and Blackrock Castle. We hunted and rambled all over the countryside.

I was educated in the North Mon and finished at 13 years of age, I will be forever grateful to the Christian Brothers for the education. They educated us and often fed us when nobody else would. My father put me into Crawford Tech and before the year was out, I fell foul of career guidance. Pop came home one Friday night with a big box and a few old tools and said: 'Here, take that down to Mick Sweeney on Monday morning and you will get the start'. So I started work as a plasterer in Christian College when they were building an extension at fourteen years of age in a short pants with a long trouser bib and brace overalls over them.

At that time, the housing situation was appalling, with people living in cramped conditions in tenement and small houses, so the native Government started to build houses and re house the people. When you look around you now and see the progress we have made, bearing in mind that at the time the State was only some thirty years old and practically broke, it was some achievement.

At seventeen, I went in search of a man's wages. I went to Walsh & Thompson builders who were looking for plasterers. I didn't accept Thompson's offer of apprentice wages. He told me I was too young to get man's wages. I made a deal with him that I'd work for the week and at the end of which, if he wasn't happy with me or thought I wasn't worth a man's wages, I'd work the week for free. He took me on after the week and paid me over the rate. Pop wasn't too pleased as I was now earning more than him!

At twenty-one, I went to England – I'd heard the money was good and the women weren't bad either. I went over with £200, spent six years there and came back with a wife, a child and £200! A fair profit! In those days, it took nine hours on the Inishfallen to Fishguard, eight hours on the train from Fishguard to London, stopping at every village in South Wales. Commercial flying didn't exist and Cork Airport wasn't then built. Air travel only got popular a number of years later and it is only in the last ten years that fares have become cheap. I worked as a plasterer in England and I did a correspondent course by night in quantity surveying and came back to Ireland and set up as a contractor. I'm still at it!

Today, I think Cork has vastly improved. It is a great city. Its multi-culturalism is bringing in new ideas. I think 99 percent of people coming to Ireland are coming to work. They are like what the Irish were in England and America, years ago now. You'd hear people talking about the good old days – 'these are the good old days'. Nowadays, in terms of the 1930s and 1940s, everyone is well off. Today everyone has good living conditions, money and work. There are social benefits for everybody.

Kay Mulcahy

With life, the glass is always half full

I was born on Seminary Road in Blackpool. The houses were small, two bedrooms and a kitchen down stairs. Life growing up in the 1950s and 1960s in Blackpool was good. We were never short of anything and my mother was a great manager. She looked after us. She knitted, sewed and cooked. My father also got stuck in. I remember my father on several occasions cooking the Sunday dinner. On one occasion, my mother was walking home with her friend and my father came to the door in his best and pressed Sunday suit and wearing an apron – she was mortified!

My grandmother's house was my second home and we had great support. I went to Saint Vincent's Convent School and we learned everything through Irish, which put me off my studies! We learned English, Irish, Maths, History and Geography. Cookery, sewing and knitting were also taught and that's where my love of knitting comes from.

I remember we played on the street games such as pickey, shop, house and school. My favourite game was playing ball – throwing three tennis balls against the wall, it was great for developing co-ordination. Skipping was also fun, we were always active. We also used to read from the *Bunty*. As a teenager and up to nineteen, I lived with my grandmother and I had to be in by eleven every night… even when I was going with my future husband, John. He had a car when I started going with him and there was a spot on Watercourse Road where we would always met. I used to give my brother my bike to go and check if he was there for our date. John and I got married young and had children at a young age. I try to live an active life and I love going to Adult Education Courses. My favourite one was in the School of Commerce on knitting and cookery.

Stella Barry

Unchained Melodies

I was born in Willis Arch by Collins Barracks in Cork. My father was from Tullamore and my mother from Dublin. They married and came down to Cork. I made friends with the children of the soldiers and I spent a lot of time playing in the barracks. My first memory as a child is going to the old Saint Patrick's National School and meeting my teacher, Ms. Hayes. I remember an open fire in the classroom and the mice running across the floor! I had a happy childhood with lots of friends and loads of games to play. There were nine in my family, so there was always something happening. It was pure simplicity – we played all day

long, games such as gobs and glassey alleys. I remember my best friend Aileen and I when were twelve, we used to play in the back room of the Belleview Bar. The lady that owned it was related to Aileen. She allowed us to put on short plays and we would dress up and charge a penny to the other kids to come in. We'd do our party pieces, they were happy memories. Then my best friend Aileen went to live in Dublin when her father was promoted in the army. I was about eleven and when she left, that was the saddest day of my life. At that time, it was expensive to go on the train to Dublin. So I didn't see her for a year after she going.

Everybody has a decade that they love. I have fabulous memories as a teenager in the sixties. At sixteen, I worked in Booth and Fox on Emmett Place and I was introduced to many new people. We used to go the Cavalier and Cavern Club, both of which were on Coburg Street. When I was eighteen, my parents allowed me to go to the Arcadia. I have great memories going to the 'Arc' on Saturday night. We'd have a long or short fur coat with flowers in our hair with gypsy style clothes. The sixties was a very peaceful, loving era in Ireland, more than this decade. The music was great and you'd be talking about the Saturday night for the week afterwards.

If you were down in the 'Arc' before ten o' clock, you were allowed in for five shillings. I remember Rory Gallagher playing who was the main man of the moment supported by other smaller bands. I met my husband whilst dancing in the City Hall. He was in the Dawn Show Band and after the gig, he came off stage and asked me to dance with him. That was it – I went out with him. I travelled around with the other five members of the group and their girlfriends to local places such as Youghal, Redbarn and the Majorca in Crosshaven, Macroom and Killarney. I remember my boyfriend, Ger (later to become my husband) playing in the Cavalier Club one night and Rory Gallagher was playing the same night. Rory's guitar had been stolen in Dublin the night before and he asked Ger could he borrow his. He played his session on it and then he came to chat to us afterwards. Sure, we were delighted to talk to him; to me he was my idol.

Ciara Murphy

I Don't Have a Title to My Story

I don't like my teachers. I am in fifth class in the North Presentation National School. If they are odd they take it out on us. That's unfair… I live in the Glen. I like Cork but I don't like all the building. It's just really annoying looking at building sites all the time. All the tractors and diggers wake you up in the morning and at the weekend at seven o' clock. My favourite place in the world is my Nan's house near the North Mon. My Nan is very kind to me. She gets me presents and looks after me… I come to The Knitting Map three times a week and I think

it is brilliant and very artistic. I like knitting but my hands get very sore after a while.

I think my Mum is great. I love her style. Her clothes are nice and funky. I have two brothers, Ian and David and a step-sister, Clodagh. I fight a lot with my brothers but it's only messing – we don't allow each other in our rooms. We always fight over that. I like swimming, tennis and tae kwon do, which I have my green belt in. What makes me really happy is when I get compliments. What makes me really sad is when someone in my family dies. My granddad died last year and my uncle died three years ago. I didn't go to school for two weeks over my granddad. I tried not to think about it for a while. That helped when I went back to school. When I'm older I'd like to be a hairdresser.

Marion Sheehan

Rhythms of Life

I was reared by my parents and my Grandaunt, who I called Nan. She reared my Dad. His mother died at child-birth with him. She was a hard worker and used to work in the Coal Quay. She was a shrewd business woman and had a great mind. When we were small, we used to spend our eight weeks summer holidays in Kerry. My mother was from Neenenare, outside Duagh in Kerry. My mother didn't have to buy food for those weeks. We were self sufficient on the farm. My dad took

three weeks holidays from Dunlops each year. There were three shifts in Dunlops and he was a hard worker. He worked there for over 23 years and I remember him being laid off in Dunlops and not getting a redundancy. Those were tough times.

I was brought up in a Corporation house in Churchfield, then moved to John Street and then to Dublin Hill. . My first memories as a child were when I was two and a half. I had to go to the North Infirmary with a kidney problem. I remember standing in the cot crying. No parents were allowed in, it was traumatic. I remember the Lee Baths – that's where half of Cork learned to swim. The water was bitter cold but it was spotlessly clean and there was a diving board. I remember jumping off the Shaky Bridge and the 'Collie' who patrolled Fitzgerald's Park. We went to Murphy's rock to fish for torneens, picked blackberries and slogged apples. Sometimes my mother used to make apple tarts out of the apples and blackberry jam. We bought Tanora and we'd pick up the glass bottles on the street and bring them to the shop and get money. It was a type of recycling, they were ahead of their time.

It's great to have great family and great friends. You have to help people out. Dolores is my best friend for twenty years. We never fell out and we both work in Yves Rocher in Dublin Hill. Today, I think there are great opportunities for young people, especially in education. My two daughters, Emma and Mary can work through the summer and earn a wage to help them get through college. I think Cork is a very cosmopolitan city. Myself and my friend Dolores were walking last night and the city we observed was like Paris... Cork is a very different city to twenty years ago. People were sitting outside and all the young ones dressed up. Drink and drugs frighten me. I fear for my two school-going daughters.

Eithne Farr

Glimpses into the Past

It all happened very quickly. I met my husband in October, got engaged at Christmas and we were married the following August. I was brought up in Ringaskiddy. I remember being on the first boat from Brittany to Ringaskiddy with the Passage West Choir. I remember being twenty and the Rural Electrification coming to Carrigaline and the surrounding areas. I can recall hanging around with strangers – the electricians from Donegal and Sligo. I did a bit of a line with one guy from Sligo. We went dancing and met up with other friends. I went to Skerry's College As a past-time, I used to travel around with a work colleague, Tom, who used to film events such as the local hunt, a fire and other sporting occasions to display to the public. We went to Dunmanway, Crosshaven and the Assembly Rooms. We had an old Hudson car with a sunroof and we had the screen out through the boot in the back.

I'm into politics and I stood for the local town council in Passage. It was breaking new ground. There were ten men and myself going up. I canvassed the whole countryside and I got a good reaction from local women. My interest was in providing facilities for children. After all that, the nine men got back in. I can still remember being so wound up about the nine men being elected. I have always been involved in voluntary work, especially the guides in Passage West and with Gorta and Cerebral Palsy. We could do with more volunteers.

Kay O' Riordan

How Lucky I am in Life

I was born and raised in Midleton in the 1920s. My first memory as a child was going to Ballycotton every year, in the first fortnight of July. We stayed in Fossett's Hotel in Ballycotton and spent much time walking on the beach in Ballytrasna. I remember making my Holy Communion. I was an only daughter (with two brothers) and I got beautiful white shoes with silver buckles. In January of that year, I remember my house caught fire as well the buildings around us. We were all bundled out…I remember our piano out in the middle of the road – that was traumatic, we spent two years living in another house.

I went to Midleton Primary School and Saint Mary's High School. I then went nursing in 1945 to Waterford Hospital, a semi-private institution. I did most of my training and spent a year in Saint Patrick's Hospital in Waterford. I left in May 1949 and I got married at 21 in July. My husband, Pat and I lived in Glasheen Road in Cork. I had two sons, John and Gerard.

Pat earned fifteen pounds, fifteen shillings as a salesman. This was a large wage but was very little when you had to take into account paying for a flat and also the suits he wore – he had to be well dressed, special jackets and shirts. As a family, we managed away fine through the years. We weren't blessed with any of the modern gadgets we have now. We made our own fun and had a very happy marriage. I remember we had two bikes and we cycled everywhere. The doctors and priests were really the only people who had a car. We even cycled to Youghal and stay a couple of days and cycled back again. We stopped at Knockaderra Lake in East Cork for a picnic. My boys have been great. Ger for his twenty-first birthday didn't want a party. He wanted to go to rugby match in Wales. From there, he went onto to Israel where he met his wife to be, who was from Norway. They fell in love and as she wished to convert from Lutheranism to Catholicism, they were chosen to get married in Rome by the late Pope John Paul II.

Religion is important to me, I am a devout Christian and I enjoy it and live on it. You have to cling onto something. My husband passed away fourteen years ago but he is still with me in spirit. I always pray to him and have faith in him... Pat was a very kind man and I remember when he died a sympathiser noted he was a man that smiled from his heart not his face. After my husband died I joined the friends of the Regional Hospital. I loved it but in recent years I have had to give it up due to health reasons. I am happy with the simple things in life. There have been tragedies in my life. At times it was not easy but I try to bounce back. I tell people to be happy and believe in themselves, be true to themselves. To enjoy what you have and not to look for the sun, moon and stars.

Rachel O' Mahony

Past, Present and Future

I grew up in Fairhill and went to North Presentation Secondary School. As a child, I remember taking my first steps. I grew up with all my neighbours' kids playing with me, but many of them have changed so much. Some of them have grown into murderers, drug dealers and rapists. When I was younger, I remember looking up to my neighbour who was a hairdresser and wanting to be like her. I also look up to my Mam and Dad. I enjoy meeting new people, making new friends… my boyfriend. I don't like people constantly nagging me and I'm not a morning person! The city has changed so much over the years, new houses, new buildings – those big changes are things to be concerned with.

Katrina Forde

I Did it My Way

I was born and bred in Killavullen near Mallow on a farm with my brother and sister. Country life was very sheltered and the three of us grew up with each other. To go to the neighbours to play was a big ordeal when they were nearly two miles away. One of my first memories as a child concerns a friend of mine in a wheelchair. She came to my house every two months and we made clothes for our dolls upstairs out of scrap material and wedding dresses for our Barbie dolls. I can remember going from a small national school to a large secondary school. I remember being called a 'culchie', that's not a nice memory. And since I always had to get the country bus home, I couldn't do any of the after school activities.

My plan after leaving school was to become a chef or to do catering. After my Leaving Cert, I went to a home economics school for a year. I didn't enjoy it the cooking for big groups, it was too regulated. I then decided to pursue art and sewing and that's where I still am today. I can now be more creative and I am happy with my job. You only have one life and I'll say no when I need to say so. I like working in the Gurranbraher-Knocknaheeny Training Centre sharing my skills with the students. It's also great to get out of the classroom and come to The Knitting Map to meet new and interesting people.

Fergal Crowley

Survival

I grew up in Rockboro Avenue on Cork's southside and have been there all my life. In my younger days, there were less cars on the road and the horse and cart was a common sight delivering the milk and bread. As a young fellow, it was the war years and I grew up before the advent of television. Going to the cinema was a big treat. I got enjoyment out of simpler things.

One of my earliest memories was as a small boy staying in a house in Ballycotton in East Cork, looking out to the lighthouse and sea and seeing a floating war mine. While we were there, the news came in that they were to detonate it and we moved to Midleton for the day. My favourite memory as a child was the summer holidays in West Cork. I had aunts and uncles who lived in Bantry and they had a farm, over a hundred acres in size. In those times, they had no electricity but oil lamps. I remember the local farmers going to the creamery with their horses and carts and they'd meet the neighbours and have a good chat. I can recall going down to Bantry on the West Cork train. During the war years, the fuel for the train was turf, so it was slow going. My family and I then got a hackney to our cousin's farms. In those days, people visited each other more.

I went to school in Ardfoyle in Ballintemple and was taught by the missionary nuns there. I remember one family who came to school by pony and trap. We got a

good religious and educational foundation there. In 1945, I moved to Presentation College on Western Road. It was a good school with a particular interest in rugby. I stayed there for nine years and then went to a private school under the auspices of Mr O' Sullivan on the South Mall. I went to the School of Commerce for a time and then started in the Munster Arcade in 1955. It was old-fashioned drapery shop. Both my parents had worked and had met there. My father had begun to work there in 1901. My parents remembered the burning of Patrick's Street and the Arcade in December 1920 and the temporary premises used on Pembroke Street by the G.P.O. in the aftermath of the burning. My father went on to spend 65 years in the Munster Arcade, he had started at the age of 14.

I can remember my first pay packet in the Arcade, one pound eleven and tuppence a week. It was small wages. I then moved to the haberdashery, very unsuitable for a young man, because we had to sell ladies requirements! We also sold wool and reels of thread and we did a good wool trade. I can recall at least three wool shops in Cork, Collins of Cook Street, Moore's Wool of the Winthrop Arcade and O' Flynn's of Castle Street. I remember in the Munster Arcade if we were out of a particular wool that a customer was looking for, we would go to another shop and acquire it. There was a tailoring section in the Arcade and I spent a time there serving customers with suits and school and business uniforms. I then moved to men's outfitting section where I spent many years.

In 1970, The Munster Arcade were taken over by the House of Frasier. In January 1978, Penneys who had been based at Queen's Old Castle, bought the Munster Arcade. I was fortunate during all those changes my job was secure and I retired in 2001 having served 46 years in the one building, so between my father and I, we had worked nearly one hundred years in the one building. I have found my retirement great. I have travelled a good bit of the globe. Last year, I toured South America with a group and I have also got as far as North America. I loved Canada, its lakes and mountains and foliage during September – one aspect that must be said, I find that Cork lacks green spaces to appreciate. I don't miss my work, retirement was a change in routine; you just move on. For years, I have been involved in the South Parish Historical Society, Saint Joseph's Young Priest's Society, the Retired People's Network and of course, looking after my garden.

Theresa Kelleher

My Faith

When I found the red door and going into the hallway, I nearly fainted. I was inside in a hallway that I had lived in as a child. It brought back so many memories for me as a child. When I got the call first about being involved in The Knitting

Map, I was interested and went down to the office of The Knitting Map and *halflangel* on Oliver Plunkett Street… In my younger years, in the 1940s, I grew up with my family and my aunt in that space.

The old narrow stairs with the banister, going up and around, were still there and as children we ran up and down those stairs for so many hours. I was one of eight children and I remember her going into Cashes, my mother in her shawl and she looking at all the Aran jumpers. Even without a proper education, she could pick up how to do the stitches by just looking at the jumpers. I could knit by the age of four and we would sit knitting by the fire. A gentleman employed my mother to knit the Aran sweaters that he could send them away to America. She would knit an Aran coat for the sum of ten shillings. We also started knitting Aran sweaters for Christy O' Mahony in Blarney.

On the ground floor, there was a man who used to do plumbing, over him lived Mr Kilgrew who owned a toy shop on North Main Street. If we ever met Mr Kilgrew in the house, he would let us in to his room which was an Aladdin's cave – from the floor to the ceiling there were boxes and boxes of toys, books, board games. That was a great feeling, we lived in very poor times. Our mother used to pay him a shilling a week saving for a toy coming up to Christmas. We had the third floor…it was a large room with a smaller room off it with a bed and cooker – you slept, ate and you cooked in this one room. Every Saturday night, there would be a big pot of bodice or ribs boiling all day long. It was luscious to eat.

There was a window, which looked down over the yard and you could lift up the old sash window and look out on Hosfords and you could see horses being kept. I can still smell the horses… Across the other side of the road was the English Legion. Up over that, there was a very small attic, where my uncle and his daughter and her children lived. My aunt used to work in the Oyster Tavern for many years, especially when the Savoy Cinema was open. All the film stars if they ever arrived in Cork used to go the Tavern and she had a book of all their autographs.

We went out and played on Oliver Plunkett Street and through the English Market and it was a paradise. You might get an apple or an orange. Once a week without fail, we would call in to see Holy Nellie of Holy God in the Good Shepherd Convent. She was our saint… you don't hear much of her now especially with the Convent closed. We went to the open air baths in the Lee Fields and Fitzgerald's Park. I remember jumping from the Shaky Bridge into the river. It was our playground and you could go out in the morning and your mother didn't have to worry about you till tea time… They were extraordinary times.

I married a great man and we settled down through the help of the Credit Union in Mayfield. I had been working in Dwyer's on Washington Street when I had my first boy, Glen. Soon after I had my second boy… and then the nightmares began. I had to travel to Crumlin, Dublin for fifteen years, he was very sick. I thought I only had a loan of him – all I could do was pray and light a candle to Our Lady. He is living in Galway now, working as a civil engineer and is very healthy. I was so thankful with God that my boy was left with me. I wanted to give something back. I got involved in setting up the Mayfield Community Shop Saint Vincent de Paul. At the time, new houses were built in the area. People were put into box-like houses like cattle. Our group tried to fill the gap of poverty and aimed to give the affected people school uniforms and shoes. There was a teacher, Ms O' Sullivan, who also started a breakfast room in Saint John's Boys National School. She was a beautiful woman in spirit.

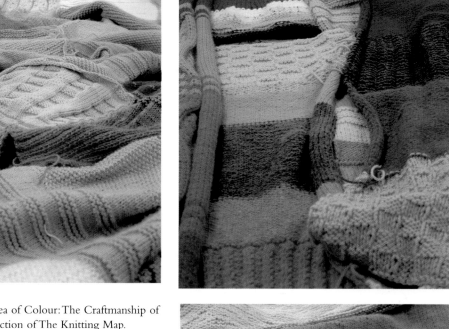

A Sea of Colour: The Craftmanship of
a Section of The Knitting Map.

Above: Community Spirit, from left to right:
Maura O' Callaghan, Anna O' Leary, Rose
McGuire, Maura O' Connell, Nuala O'
Donovan and Maureen O'Leary.

Left: Left to right, from the top: Jane
Duggan, Rose Conlon, Barbara Bruen, Elsie
O' Connell

Knit-in at Cork 2005 House on 28 February 2004, Pope's Quay. Valerie Byrne, Cork 2005 Project Manager on the left is applauding the efforts.

Knit-in at Cork 2005 House, Pope's Quay in February 2004 with Jools Ellis-Gilson on the left setting the scene.

Workshop team at Colaiste Choilm, in Spring of 2004.

Workshop group at Blarney Girls National School, Co. Cork in Spring of 2004.

Workshop team at Niche (Northside Community Health Initiative), Cork in Spring of 2004.

Workshop team at Cois Tine, Cork in Spring 2004.

Workshop team in August of 2004 at Cope Foundation, Cork.

Knit-in at Cork Sexual Violence Centre, Spring 2004.

Workshop team at Gurranabraher-Knocknaheeny Training Centre, Spring 2004.

Cope Foundation members at the Knit-in at Merchants Quay Shopping Centre, Cork in Spring 2004.

The Knitting Map stand during the Day of Welcomes, St. Patrick's Street, Cork on 1 May 2004.

The workshop team at Shandon Craft Centre, Cork in Spring 2004.

Knit-in at Cork Vision Centre, 29 April 2004.

Above: Jools Ellis-Gilson on Daunt's Square, Cork enthusing the masses.

Knit-ins on Cork buses.

Knit-in at Fota House, Cork on 1 August 2004.

Knit-in/ knit-on bikes, 25 September 2004 with Sue Tector-Sands on the left and Kate O'Brien on the right.

Mary Goggin on the right checks out the mode of transport!

Knit-in at the R.D.S., Dublin in November of 2004.

Knit-in at St. Finbarre's Cathedral in November 2004.

Knit-in at Cork City Gaol in December 2004.

The official launch of The Knitting Map at the Cork 2005 House on 15 January 2005.

The Pied Piper workshop through the streets of Cork on 28 July 2005.

The Pied Piper workshop with Marian O' Sullivan on St. Patrick's Street.

Entertaining the masses on the Pied Piper Workshop, from left to right: Dave Carville, Elizabeth O' Dea, Evelyn Quinlan, Katie Nally and Julie Kelleher.

Mad Hatter Day on 13 August 2005, from left to right: Caroline Kearney, Barbara A. Bruen, Una Long, Mary Norris, Marian O' Sullivan, Jackie Magnin, Elsie O' Connell and Julianna Griffin.

Chapter 3

The Architecture of Life

'Life can be difficult. I find it a trial, all day everyday. Sometimes I must pull back and need my own space and tranquillity. I don't do enough of it' (Barbara A. Bruen)

Barbara A. Bruen

Living Memories

I remember as a child my freedom and my happiness within my family and my home. There was much going on in our house. We had a nice garden and eighteen acres. I had great freedom. I could come and go. If I wanted to be on my own, I could go down the field alone with just the cows. I loved the nature of it. I lived opposite Blackrock Castle in Castlemahon in the fifties. I always remember the plaque on the side of the house, built in 1798, which was the year of the rising. The house is now a nursing home. There are now houses built on the land and when we had it there was nothing there but the big fields. We enjoyed our family life there. We played golf in the front fields with my father and we had a tennis court in the back. Over the years, he built us a swimming pool. There was always something exciting happening and there was plenty time for playing. We had a lovely vegetable garden. We all were given jobs to do. I went to school in the Ursulines and we often biked there. I enjoyed sports, golf tennis and hockey and in particular, I enjoyed being part of a team. I am an outdoor person to this day and I like open spaces. I live in Midleton now.

I love helping and meeting people. I often help Cork 2005 by bringing booklets of the events and passing them out in Midlelton and getting people to come up to events in Cork. I am always knitting on the bus and I tell people about the Map. I work with Cork Environmental Forum. I did a stand in a three-day environmental event with the Co-op in Midleton. I am involved with the food and wine event in Midleton every year. I volunteer with the Jazz Festival and I look after some of the artists playing. I also help out with the Early Spring Festival in Midlelton.

Those events get me out and I have great enjoyment meeting all different types of people.

I have never married. It would not be from trying too hard. I have always been too busy. I have never been in the right place. All the good men are gone. They are all married! I want to meet someone who will be interested in me for the person I am. I find it hard to meet someone who is interested in me in that way.

I enjoy music, knitting, embroidery, dress-making and I sew beads onto my dresses to enhance my clothes. It's the way I am, I'm a creative person and I like to design. I make use of my talents. A number of years ago, I became friendly with a neighbour of mine, Eleanor Longfield, in Blackrock. She had a broken hip and she became ill. We were good friends. She was very good with her hands especially doing crochet and weaving on spinning wheels. We had something in common and she asked me to help her. Eleanor came out of Castle Mahon for a time but got ill and was moved to Saint Patrick's Hospital. I remember on Saint Patrick's Day, she sat up and said: 'Barbara, will you bring me home to Hove in England?' I agreed to her request. I got in touch with her solicitor in England. She knew the nursing home in Hove. We took a flight to London and taxied from London to Hove. I stayed with her for four days and I then had to come home; I cried my eyes out leaving her. It was sad to leave her but I was content that she was happy to be home. To be able to do something like that is really rewarding – to be able to help someone to the best of your ability. I have nursed many wonderful people. To be

able to give of yourself in all that you do – the garden, knitting, sewing – friends. I am a giver. When you give, you will find life very rewarding. You should give of your best, be honest and respectful. We're all human and we all make errors. Don't judge people. I am not a judge. I can be really hard on myself at times.

Life can be difficult. I find it a trial, all day everyday. Sometimes I must pull back and need my own space and tranquillity. I don't do enough of it. The best place for me is down by the sea. I am off the cigarettes and I have much more energy now than I used to have. There is always something to be done.

My father was a great man for doing things perfectly and I was brought up that way. I lost my dad 33 years ago… He got a heart attack… It had a terrible affect on me and all the family. He was there one minute and gone the next. We never had a chance to say goodbye. Everybody looked up to my father. He was a well-known figure in the golfing world. I didn't know how great a person he was and it was only when he died that his greatness as a person was missed. As a father, I was very close to him and lived my life knowing that he is close to me spiritually. I have always found a way to get on with my life and I have done it through my creativity and my interests. You are living every day to the fullest, making history. You make memories and I pick out the great, living memories… It keeps me living.

Margaret O' Rourke

Back to Front: Three Phases in a Life

If I wrote my own biography, the title would have to be: 'Three Phases in a Life'. I spent the first eighteen years with my parents. I spent the second eighteen years raising three children. I have spent the third eighteen years going back to education, which perhaps I should have done in the second phase. I am not sure if I have gone forwards or backwards in my life. I made a list of things I wanted to do before I was fifty. One of them was at some future stage to go back to education. I went to school at the Presentation Convent in Doneraile. They gave us our books for a year and I loved reading. When I did my Leaving Cert, unfortunately I didn't go on to any further education in College but what I did do was get married and have three kids. Whilst living in Cork, I saw an ad in the paper in 1994 for Coláiste Stiofáin Naofa and I went out and did a short course and then a long course in tourism and heritage, which included folklore, history and archaeology.

In January 1995, I was encouraged to apply to do Arts in U.C.C. and went on to do a B.A. in Folklore and English. You have to take folklore up in second year. Gearóid Ó Crúalaoích inspired me in the Folklore department. I had heard him before in Colaiste Stiofáin Naofa and he inspired me to do more. He was so

interesting in U.C.C. and it was he who encouraged me to stay on and pursue a Masters of Arts.

I did my Masters on the topic of death rituals in Ireland and how it has changed over the years from the merry wake to the funeral parlour. Very seldom today that you would have someone waked at home. When I was growing up that was the normal procedure. Both my grandmothers were waked at home. My mother had a bottom drawer in her wardrobe with items and clothing that were to be used when she died; they had belonged to my grandmother – white sheets, a white bed spread and white pillow cases. It was something I grew up with. My mam used to say to me: 'Margaret, when I die, make sure I'm laid out properly'. You would think as the years went on, the drawer would be forgotten about but every summer, the clothing was aired. My mother often spoke about death and it was something that I was not afraid of.

My grandmother died when I was seven. I remember going down to the house and saying goodbye. I remember when my grandfather died and saying goodbye to him. I miss them terribly but I wasn't afraid when they died. My Masters gave me the opportunity to explore further death rituals and find out about other peoples' views on the changes from a wake – which is more personal to a funeral home – which is more impersonal and perhaps clinical. The home setting for a wake is different in the sense you can sit down and have a chat and a cup of tea and reminisce on the person who died.

For my study, I read up on the old customs. Some of them I knew myself but there were other rituals older again. The merry wake was an all-night vigil and in many cases, would transform into all night sessions of food, drinking and smoking. You can't have the family and neighbourhood staying all night in the funeral home. I looked at the way Princess Diana died and how that was taken out of all proportion with its mass moaning and hysteria. King Hussein had died about the same time and on the paper, the saddle was put on his horse back to front as well as his boots left in the stirrups, which symbolised a fallen leader. I was also interested to know about the more unusual traditions associated with death. I spoke to Pat Speight, a great storyteller in Cork who directed me to explore the idea of people coming back from the dead - ghosts.

I talked to Mrs. Forde the undertaker, a very brilliant and professional woman. We talked about what happens from the time she gets a phone-call saying someone has died to what services she provides. You don't realise how much the undertaker is involved in someone's death, from advice about the grave, coffin, flowers to how to say goodbyes personally before everyone comes into the funeral home; about coming in for ten minutes during the day when no one is there. We spoke about the advice to give if children are the bereaved – to write a letter and place it in the coffin. She gets the whole family involved in the funeral arrangements. They are professional people and play a large role in helping the family to cope with death. When you walk into a funeral home, it's something you never see – how involved the undertaker is. They have to be seen to be respectful of the dead and their family and friends. Mrs. Forde spoke about her experiences dealing with her husband dying. My entire Masters was an eye opener. Before I started my thesis, I was not in favour of funeral homes. What I learned is that you must have an open mind about life issues.

I learned a lot from the Masters. I penned ideas that I had had myself from when my grandmother died to my mother's death. Transferring ideas on how I felt was important for me. My mother had three months to live after being diagnosed with cancer. She was at home for that time and I had to be a supporting daughter. I had to walk in and be in good form, even though I knew she was dying. I also have to be respectful of the wishes she had to be dressed properly at her funeral. She wanted to be laid in her own bed properly. I did exactly what she told me to do at the end of the day. Many people cannot say they could do that; my wish is that I would like to die at home and then brought to a church.

At the moment I am happy the way I am. I am involved in Sr Kathleen's Wednesday Afternoon Club, the Social Resources Centre in Roches Buildings and with a project for Belarus, knitting blankets and slippers to send out there. I have five grand-daughters and they are five different individuals. They will put a mark on the world in different ways. My grand-daughter, Sarah just did her Leaving Certificate and is hoping to go to UCC. Another grand daughter Kerina is into road bowling and golf. She is interested in outdoor activities. This year I was very proud of her when she got an award and was picked to be involved as a volunteer with the Special Olympics. She raised a large sum of money for Special Olympians in Doneraile. My other grandchildren Taylor, Shannen and Hollie are involved in sport and they are well-defined children in their own right.

I am very proud of my three children who are grown up. They went through a lot when I was separated. I missed out on a few years of their lives. Separation in Ireland is very traumatic. It's not family-orientated and the split is not friendly. My children came through it. They still have their mother and father. My motto in life? Every morning I wake up and I make an effort to make myself happy. It's difficult but I do it seven days a week. There are days where you don't want to be happy but I try.

Mary Goggin

A Dream…Shattered

I was always a music fan – particularly of him. The first time I saw David Bowie, I saw him as very individual and many people could not understand what he was about. When I was thirteen, I thought he was brilliant. When I was fifteen, I carved his name onto my hand with a compass. People in school thought I was mad but I thought I was great! He even had his own way of writing his own name with a flash of lighting down the middle. I used to practice doing my signature like that. His record company was called *MainMan* and as far as I was concerned he was the main man. I used to write to him and when I was in England I used to stand about outside where he lived that time. One time I wrote to him and I got a reply back from his agent whose name was Stellar Steel. It was in red ink. The girls in school wouldn't believe me and they made me lick the ink to prove it was real.

David Bowie announced his retirement a couple of times. He was playing in Dublin in the Point Depot and I had never seen him in Concert and I thought I should go up there. I persuaded my sister to go up with me and we decided to stay over night. I decided I wanted to make a huge gesture to David Bowie and bought twelve red roses and took them off to the Point Depot. When we got there, our

seats were not very good. They were behind pillars. We walked down to the back of the hall and I said to my sister: 'I have to give him the flowers'. My sister refused to come up to the stage with me.

The front of the stage was full of people, people squashed and sweating. I said to myself if I didn't do it now I might never get the chance again. I crawled under people's legs, climbed over people, the railings. I got up to the front…my heart was just popping out of my mouth… I went into the middle of the stage and stood in front of it. I waited till he came over and stood in front of me…I had visions of him saying to me; *'There you are, where have you been all my life?'* I thought he would instantly recognise me, his biggest fan. He stood in front of me. I pulled my hand back with the flowers in it. I took a deep breath and I threw the flowers as hard as I could. They flew into the air… and then… into the orchestra pit. My heart was broken – he never even knew I existed.

Una Long

I Can Die Happy Now

I love America but I wouldn't live there. I think their pace of life is reckless. They work from morning to night, six days a week. They travel long distances to get to work everyday. They come home. They don't have time to sit on the couch. They go into the shower and straight to bed. They have loads of money but they must plan ahead with their lives. It is a different type of lifestyle and culture to ours. Their extremes of weather are another problem, very cold to very hot. I am just back from Cape Cod – 93/95° F. Our blood was not thinned out for that kind of heat. We stayed in the Irish village and the food was wonderful there. You could have a five course meal if you wanted to every evening. Their food portions are large. Americans are larger than life – that's what I love about them. They are very literal to the word and accurate. If they tell you it's ten paces to some place, it is ten paces to walk. I love their honesty.

Corrupt is a word I'm using for Ireland at the moment, corrupt from the top down. I think there is much misdoings going on in hierarchical orders of people. Our younger generation are being disillusioned by the people they should be looking up to. Every week, there is something coming up in the news – the Gardaí, tribunals, clergy. I was raised in a time when you were down in church every week and go down on your knees confessing your sins. You had to wear an item over your head going into the church. You had the Latin Mass. I am a Minister of the Word in my church. The priests in my parish are lovely guys who are good and solid in their community, but they have all been tarred with the same brush, so that the youngsters of today are saying: 'God – there's no God there'.

I'll tell you another story, which will take me off on a tangent again. A neighbour of mine two years ago lost her baby. She was killed by accident. A whole family and community were affected. Her parents and her in-laws were also living quite close. The incident touched everybody in the community. What she didn't know is that she was four months pregnant at the time and when she reached her sixth month, she lost that child. That was two babies dead in a couple of weeks…she was devastated. The family was torn apart by the tragedy and blame was passed from person to person, the term Act of God was mentioned. The light at the end of the tunnel is that she had a little boy a couple of weeks ago – but how will she come

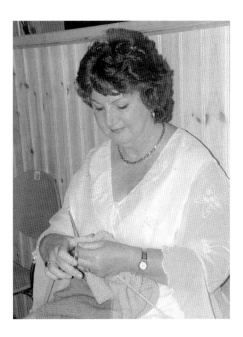

out of it at the other end? Will she be over-protective? Will the child be marred? Will there be another generation destroyed? Those are tragedies that you would ask – where is God now? Why would he tear that family apart and give them all those troubles? Those incidents have no direct affect on me but I think they are important in my life. They do make me think about God and where is he?

My first memory as a child was with an aunt of mine on Richmond Hill. I bonded very well with her as a child. My father during the fifties was a carpenter and there was very little work in Cork and he got on the boat like a lot of men at the time and went to Fords in Dagenham. My mother said she would join him and try to make a home in England. As it turned out, nine weeks is all she could bear, as she was so homesick. My aunt looked after me while my mother was abroad. In that nine weeks, I must have bonded very well with my auntie. I remember sitting on the table and she washing me down (as there was no bathrooms) and getting me dressed in the mornings and having tomato sauce at the side of the plate of my dinner.

After my mother returned to Cork, we lived in a two-roomed tenement house in Leitrim Street in Blackpool, with no electricity and the toilet in the yard. My mother was pregnant when she came back from England and I had a brother, Jim. We got one of the new Corporation houses – a bungalow in Churchfield which even had a bathroom with no toilet bucket! Our new house faced onto O' Leary's Field and you could see the harbour. My father came home two or three times a year to visit and he sent on money by telegram. He was sending on twice the wage of a worker in Cork. It was hard on my mother rearing two of us with him away. My mother was from a family of twelve and they all lived close-by to offer support. She was always optimistic. She ran social events such as bingo in the parochial hall. She also set up meals-on-wheels in Churchfield. She was a great influence on my life.

The notion of community is important to me. When I was young, there would always be someone coming in and out to see my mother. I started off my adventures in community development in Mayfield with the Adult Literacy Scheme. I saw an advertisement on a local newsletter called *Focus* looking for volunteers. I went to a meeting and was opted onto the steering group. That was my first entrance back to work outside the home. It took me a while to get used to the procedures of etiquette of meetings. I became a tutor and also took an interest in Dyslexia. There was very little information on how to deal with adults and dyslexia.

As well as the Community Development Project, I am involved in Mayfield Community Adult Learning Project and Mayfield Employment Action Project. I got an offer of going to college to pursue a Community Education and Development Degree at CIT. I did weigh up everything especially how it would affect my family and home. I got my degree. I specialised in Computer Skills, Quark Express and the European Driving Licence. The skills I learned I am now using with the magazine, *Mayfield Matters*.

My Mum, a great inspiration in my life

My life is full to capacity and I suppose I can now die happy. My husband, Brendan and I had five children, one girl and four boys, now all grown up. I buried one boy as a baby. I am taking time presently to enjoy my three grandchildren, they are very important to me. I see a difference in me and how I deal with my grandchildren as opposed to dealing with my own children. I have far more patience and I have far more time to give them. I love when they visit. I can do the nice bits and then pack them off home! My life motto? Live in the moment, focus on the now… but I think that came with maturity.

Margaret Kingston

Mix and Match

I'm originally from the Corporation buildings in the inner city, off the Coal Quay. Everybody was in the same boat growing up in the fifties, we didn't have much. We lived in a flat, my brother, my mam, my uncle and I. Growing up, there was much poverty on the Coal Quay side. We were lucky; we didn't have the Frank McCourt style poverty. I went to Saint Peter and Paul's School with a good Catholic upbringing in the church across the way. I didn't like school and I looked forward to leaving it at the age of fourteen. You could go on and do your Leaving Certificate but it wasn't as big a thing as it is today. The School of Commerce was one option available to me. I did the exams because many of my friends did

them and when they did not get into the same class as me, I opted out. I was then obliged by law to attend the one day a week for two years in the Vocational School on Wellington Road, a red brick building by 96 F.M. today. You had to attend there whilst you went to work. The subjects included religion, needle work, dress-making and cooking.

My mother had a shop/café called the Marina Café on Kennedy Quay. The dockers would come in for tea and sandwiches. All nationalities came in and out. At that time dockers would dig the coal and shove it into buckets, which would be loaded and dumped in the coal store. Many goods were packed loose and had to be hand packed. My mum worked for Mrs. Reynolds and took the option of buying the café when the landlady died. I have a hundred and one stories from the shop days. Some of the sailors not being able to speak English… romances! I remember going out with an officer in my teens; it was a hug and a kiss, holding hands. There was nothing in it, just the box of chocolates and the going to the pictures – that's not saying temptation did not arrive. He was very romantic. He was working in Dublin and based on a ship called the *Uxbridge* bringing fertilizer into Port of Cork.

I met my husband Ernest who was checking exports and imports. When we met first, we didn't get on. I thought he had an attitude, but it was a relationship that developed – he asked me out and we ended up marrying each other. The unusual thing about our relationship was that he was Protestant and I was Catholic. Bishop Lucey was here in Cork and at the time, Ernest was obliged to convert to Catholicism. There was no major difference between the religions. I got married at nineteen and I'm now thirty-five years happily married. We moved to Military Road to great neighbours. My children are grown up and I'm very proud of them. I never went out to work. My family are now reared. The only regret I have is that it is a pity I have nothing to fall back on now at this time of my life.

I like to see people happy and like cheering people up if I can. I am a happy go lucky person anyway. Positive thinking is important. I get angry when I think of my politicians, the church – what people can get away with. I brought my children up with morals. The children today don't seem to have key morals such as respect for your elders. I feel that is coming from working parents and not giving their full time to the rearing of their children. I think television and computers are the ruination of many children.

Jackie Magnin

Finding a Home

I had always been interested in going abroad and I have seen different and beautiful places. Australia had fascinated me for years. I had read much on aspects such as the Outback, the Flying Doctor Service and school by radio. I got the opportunity in the sixties and I went from London to Sydney by plane. Flying was only getting cheap at that time. I returned to London by boat over five weeks. With eighteen hundred passengers and eight hundred crew members, the *Australis* was one of the

last liners that travelled right around the world. Due to the prevailing sea current, we travelled west to east and stopped in places such as Tahiti, Panama City, Miami and then Rotterdam. Five weeks is a long time on board. Every week, there was a variety show organised and it was the passengers that took part in it. I did the costume making, whatever was needed. It was the final show in which I took part – Greek folk dancing, but at that stage in our journey, the liner was mid Atlantic and the ship was pitching and tossing – so when you jumped, the coming down part was longer than expected !

    I was born and grew up in Rotterdam with my older brother and parents in the older part of the town. As Rotterdam was badly bombed in the first years of the World War II, the central part of the city was being rebuilt whilst I was growing up. I went to Teacher Training College and taught for one year in a primary school. I then packed my bags and went to live in Kent in England for sixteen months. That was basically a stopover before I went to live in Australia in 1968 for seven years. For two years in Sydney, I worked for the French Commercial Diplomat, house–keeping and cooking. It was interesting to see the workings of the diplomatic service on the inside. When I left that job, I found Sydney was a very expensive place to live. I was fortunate that I met and made some friends from Tasmania and spent five years there.

    In 1975, I came back to Holland, was married for a brief while and taught for most of that time. In 1988, I got a life changing experience in the form of Breast

Cancer. It was successfully operated on but the whole process marked the end of my teaching career, as teaching was too stressful. So taking my disability pension, I went on holidays with a friend in Ireland in 1991. I felt at home in Ireland and Irish music and singing were already favourites of mine over the years. It was also easy to talk to people. In 1992, I came to Ireland on my own, spent ten days in Galway and some nights in Inis Mór. I decided that Ireland was where I belonged. It was just a matter of being practical. When I was in my twenties, it was easier to pack up and go. Now in my late forties, I had very different decisions to make. I had to think about building my life up from scratch and surviving. In 1996, I settled here for good and bought a house recently in West Cork. It's what you make of the place itself, how you 'connect' into the place. Lovely neighbours, great places to walk with the dog, beautiful scenery, the atmosphere, great history; I'm living in an old house the best part of three hundred years old. I knew a few people before I settled here and found a home in West Cork. I was never home-sick for Holland all the years I was abroad. I came home and visited my parents when they were alive. Today, I now have no ties with Rotterdam but I do go back from time to time.

I enjoy Irish crafts – knitting and crochet and sewing, pottery, silverwork. Needlework was always part of my life. When I moved here, I found out about Irish lace making. I am a member of the Traditional Lace Makers of Ireland. It is important to keep crafts alive just to see if anything what they were like and to get to know the lives of the people who used to be in those crafts. I was intrigued to find out that after the Great Famine, women and young girls brought in a regular income through lace-making. Without the extreme poverty, there might not have been as much Irish lace and the associated craft surviving as there is now. The social part of the experience in great – stitching away for a day, chatting, which is very like The Knitting Map experience.

Elizabeth O' Dea

A Working Title

Cork seems more like Carlow than Dublin, more like a town. I had been to Cork a number of times. I like the geography of Cork... its pace of life. You can walk everywhere. I have never got a bus in Cork. You can walk up and down to U.C.C. and get accommodation very much central to everything or you can live up in college and have U.C.C. handy always if you want to. When I started working in Cork, it changed… it is not the same city as I perceived in College, a lot more stressful. You meet people who don't have the same goal, people pulling against each other.

I am not a homebird, but my family is very important to me. I feel if you don't go home to see how they are, you won't know how they are and they won't know

how you are. I'm from near Carlow on a small estate with 32 houses. Carlow has mushroomed a lot in recent years and our estate is surrounded by other estates. I am very attached to my home and I have stayed in contact with my school friends. I really like Carlow and would like to go back there to work with the skills I have learned. Carlow is a quiet place. It has a small cinema. There is not that much live music in pubs. There is an arts festival called Éigse. I worked with them for a time. They started out more so as a visual arts and crafts festival. There is a strong tradition of exhibiting arts and crafts in Carlow especially at Saint Patrick's the old seminary – a natural gallery. I remember before I did my Junior Cert, my friend Emma Kirwan and I cycled to all of the then handful of Éigse venues. That was it, it would take us a morning. Today it is a huge event.

Deciding about college was tough, I used to walk to school past the train station in Carlow. The train served the Waterford, Kilkenny and Dublin line. One Friday, my Leaving Cert class had a half day and I was getting annoyed with the whole C.A.O. filling out business and everyone worrying out about it. On the way home from school, I got a notion to get on the train to Kilkenny, deciding that I wasn't going to think about anything except places and courses from the time I stepped on the train to the time I stepped off it. I was going to have my mind made up …and I did…I went off to Kilkenny on my own and went to a coffee shop over a book-shop and got a whole cafeteria of coffee. I thought I was very sophisticated! I decided to do the Drama and Theatre Studies degree. I think now of the experience of the train and the finality of it, taking a notion to get on a train to decide my course that day…nobody knew where I was and that the decision was entirely in my own head.

I went to college in Cork. I always loved drama and theatre studies. My first job was with the Youth Theatre in Carlow and years before I had done school plays. I applied to the first year of the Drama and Theatre Studies in U.C.C. My Mam talked me into coming down to do the audition and interview. I was convinced that everyone applying for the course would have experience and of course when I came down, it seemed they all did, which was a horrible experience. I knew before my results of my Leaving Cert that I did pass the audition and interview stage. I had decided to come to Cork anyway because being from Carlow, you go to Dublin for everything, shopping, plays – Dublin is so close. I thought Dublin colleges were tacky. I was familiar with Dublin and it wasn't exciting or adventurous anymore. It was also the commuting factor, the idea of travelling long distances, the hassle of which I wasn't up for. Three of my friends came to Cork with me.

I drive myself to be good at things. I like to do things perfectly; I think the eldest in a family is born with those traits – more ambitious and driven. Perfection is not something I expect from others, or would even advise. My favourite quote is by Senca, a classical poet, which I have painted on the walls of our shed in Carlow: 'if you would judge, understand'. It is important for people who are perfectionists to remember that not everyone is like that and that it is not necessarily the best way to be all the time. Sometimes, you have to sit back and 'chillax'. You can't control everything and everyone and you shouldn't try.

Margaret Kennedy

Keeping the Knots Unravelled

College was new and different and in some ways it was the beginning of my life. When I was living at home, I belonged to everybody and did not see myself as my own person. I didn't recognise that until I lived away from home. I was an independent person. I could make my own decisions about things. It was the shock of moving first, being independent and not having someone looking over you…no one asking where you were going or what you were doing. Being my own person was great. I stayed in digs originally and when I found out what college life was about, it was too restricting where I was living. I moved in with some friends. I went to college in Waterford Institute of Technology to do social studies.

I went from Waterford to work in Dublin for the Health Board with children and teenagers. That was for six years. During my college years, I had completed

some work placement there. I had a gentle introduction to Dublin. I loved the buzz of the city. I was sharing with my sister. To work was great – to have money for the first time, you can go on holidays… With the job, extra responsibility came. I took a career break from my Dublin job for a year. I went travelling to Australia and New Zealand. It wasn't something I always wanted to do. I just felt it might be nice. It was very much if it happens, it happens and if it doesn't, it doesn't. The plan was to go with friends but that didn't happen. I had already applied for my visa. In the end, I went with my sister and we met people we knew out there.

We started in Perth and then went to Melbourne to Sydney. Perth was really quiet. Melbourne was busier and Sydney was a really happening place. Life was more laid back. I pushed the boat out. I did things I never did before just everyday things like working with different agencies in Sydney, like getting on a bus at six o' clock in the morning and never have worked in a particular place before and I with my map figuring out how to get to the place. Meeting so many different people was a challenge. My own circle had to be broken and I had to mix with other people. I had to broaden my network of friends. Travel broadened my mind to look at the bigger picture – to be more open to peoples' life experiences. I did the usual activities, bungie-jumping (which I hadn't done before) skiing and glacier walking in New Zealand, hot air ballooning – all new experiences.

Coming back, part of me really wanted to stay there and then another part of me wanted to get back to my life in Ireland. We landed in a cloudy Ireland at the end of August. The thoughts in my head were: 'I don't want to be here'. It took me a long time to settle again. Now I think sometimes the idea of being there would be great, but yet, I know it would be very different and not the same to go back.

When I came back, I was unsettled again. The many people I was friends with and worked with had gone. Dublin wasn't the same for me. It seemed to have become more impersonal and so anonymous. Maybe it had always been like that. Previously, I had been into a routine. I didn't notice it… I applied for jobs all over the country and I got a job in Cork; Cork was smaller than I expected. I noticed people were friendlier. People would acknowledge you on the street, which took me by surprise. When you walked into a shop, people would say something about the weather or acknowledge you in someway. That did not happen in Dublin. I could find myself settling down in Cork. I love being so close to the country. I can get a car and drive twenty minutes and I am in the country like going to Ballincollig Park or the beach. I love having the freedom to do that.

My life adventures to date have been varied and challenging. When I think of the things I have done, they might seem straightforward, but there were other obstacles there at the time. When I get an idea in my head, I like to follow it through; I like to follow my heart, moving outside my comfort zone, not getting myself tied up in knots – I like keeping the knots unravelled. People ask me – friends and family – what will I do at the end of this year? I feel they are more concerned about what I'll do next than I am. I'm not in a panic over it. I know something will come up and I'll work on it when I need to. I am doing what I want to do. I try, no matter how bad a situation is, to look on the positive side of life. Trying to do your best with a situation. I am a quiet person at heart. It does take me a while to get to open up to people or maybe people to get to know me. I do hold myself back from people. I can be a bit unsure, but I have resilience and a quiet self-confidence.

Eileen Henrick

Misadventures of Eileen Henrick

My favourite memory was holidays in Weaver's Point, Crosshaven when I was a child. I loved the freedom. We went down there every summer to my grandmother's house. All my cousins would come down. We never went on our own. An aunt always came with her children. We a great time, climbing the rocks and picking the blackberries in the field. We would walk down to the merries – great stuff.

The first girlie sun holiday was brilliant. Seven of us went away to Tenerife. We were just silly for a whole week. I have to say since I have been thirty, life gets

better and better. From The Knitting Map and meeting people, I have decided to go back to College to do social studies. I like socialising, going out having a drink, just chatting and having a laugh. I like meeting people. I try and have fun the best I can, but that's something I have learnt with age.

Meeting my partner Kevin was fun. It was the first time I dated in fourteen years. I had met him some years ago. Dating was like been sixteen all over again. It was horrible but in a nice way. It was very exciting and very weird but you're also very vulnerable. At sixteen you're very vulnerable, that what's I felt like. It took ages to get the courage to date, to get the courage to actually go out for a meal and aspects like that. Seven years on, I am still seeing him. It's not easy for people to date in Cork. I have single friends who don't find it easy. They find it hard enough to meet people. Many of the people I know end up dating people they already know. It is difficult to go out there and no one wants to go out there looking for a relationship. You don't want to go out and say: 'I want to meet someone tonight'. You want to go out and have fun. I think you don't meet people going to clubs and pubs.

Francis McCarthy

And What I am Going to do Tomorrow?

Home is where my family is – that can be in any country. I grew up near Ottawa, Canada. My father was an English Professor. I studied astronomy and physics. I knew that I couldn't get my teacher's degree because of my college marks. I came to England looking for a job. I met my husband in England. I met him in a late night club in North London. He was Irish, from Monkstown in Cork and working in Poole. I met him in 1987 and waited, I followed him around the world! He got a job in the States, so I moved back to Canada. I did my teaching degree. We spent two and half years in different countries and travelling twelve hours to see each other, from near Lake Ontario to Virginia in D.C.

We moved to England to where we could both work – this was the guy for me. He is a genuinely nice guy, we're as smart as each other, we have the same sense of humour. I said to the women in Monkstown that they were not only blind but stupid that they let him get away! He is the social core of his group. He has friends that he knows since school and he is still part of a close-knit circle of lads whose parents stayed in the village. They all come back every Christmas to the village.

During our travels, I visited his mum in Monkstown. Jonathan told me as we flew in watch out for the cows near the runway. We came in over Cork harbour and he was able to show me his house in Monkstown. We're landing at the airport

and I'm saying where is the airport? With Heathrow you can see the airport and the buildings…you fly into Cork and you're looking at fields of cows. It was March. I couldn't get over the lush green landscape… I loved it. Driving on the other side of the road was interesting. We arrived in Monkstown, settled in and went out to meet his friends. One guy I could not understand his thick Cork accent. I'd smile and nod and get the translation later – it took me four years to be able to understand him!

The decision to leave the States was based on an annual holiday to Ireland at Christmas, Jonathan had to see his friends and family. His close-knit structure in the States was not enough. Cork was also closer to his friends in London. Ireland is the fourth country I have lived in, even my family moved from Canada to Cork.

There are things about Cork I love but those are things that lead me to hate the place too. I can't get a job here. I am applying for jobs and getting nowhere because of the fact I am not from Cork. To come in as an outsider, it is very hard to be accepted. There is the feeling that Cork looks after its own. The city should be more open. Carrigaline has a population which is increasing in size in huge numbers, they are not all from Ireland. There is a lot of English people settling there and working the pharmaceutical companies in Ringaskiddy, even Irish people are returning home. There is a good education system for children. You are only going through life once, so enjoy it, don't dwell on the past, keep looking to the future. Grab it, don't let it approach you. I created my own world in Cork.

Sally O' Neill

Pride of my Life

Everybody knew one another, who your mother and father were, a tight-knit group of people. I was born in Waterford City in 1949 and I grew up in a small terrace house with no front garden, in a time when neighbours looked out for one another. Many of them were older middle-aged women and we were a young family. As children we went to the shop for them and they always treated us well and we always looked out for them.

My mother is a Co. Kilkenny woman and when she came to Waterford to work, she met and married my dad. They rented or lodged as they called it then with a lady and her husband whom I adopted as my Nanny and Daddy Fannin. I would often ramble into their part of the house. Mam, Dad and I lived with them until I was about three or so. I never thought I would live anywhere else. Nanny lived in No 2 and when Mam and Dad moved to No 6, I spent most of my time in No 2, only going home when my Dad was due home from work. I ate all my meals with Nanny Fannin and when I started school, I would stop at their house on my way

home. I collected their milk in a jug from the local dairy every day. Daddy Fannin was getting old by the time I was at school and he was unable to see. I would take him by the hand and lead him to the cobbler's shop where he sat chatting for an hour or so. I would then collect him and walk him home for tea.

Nanny and Daddy Fannin ran a small shop. They sold bread, cakes, bundles of sticks, paraffin oil and other odds and ends. After school, I would be sent to Nanny's for the bread. Once a week, we would get a cake called a slab. It was a kind of layer cake with pink icing sprinkled with coconut. As our family grew, the slice got smaller! My father was orphaned at a young age and when his family came along especially myself who was the oldest, we were important to him. He doted on us all and made each one of us feel that we were the only ones that mattered.

There were seven boys and seven girls in our family. My mum was a brilliant hard worker at home trying to look after us all. Dad was a huge influence on my life. We had everything we needed but it did fall to Dad to give us all the attention. My Mum loved us in her way. I remember my father's sense of fun. He had a little wooden seat on the bar of his bike and he would take me out to Tramore. I remember winning goldfishes and bringing them home in the plastic bags. I wonder sometimes where were the rest of my brothers and sisters. I don't remember them. They must have been smaller. I remember years later my family going by train to Tramore and my dad and I on the bike.

One of the strongest memories of my Dad was when my Dad was coming home from work, watching him coming up the road. We'd go down and meet him. My parents called me Sally after my dad's mother. He also sang the song: 'Sally, Pride of our alley... don't ever wander away from the alley from me'. He sang it at every family event for me, even if I wasn't there! A number of years ago, Maxi of R.T.E. was doing a programme about songs and what they mean to us, I sat down and wrote about my lovely Dad and the kind of person he was and how much he meant to us. Maxi picked my story and played *Sally*... I cried so much.

I remember as a child my father going to Africa with the army in the early fifties. I remember my mother, Nanny Fannin and myself standing at the quays in Waterford seeing my dad off and mother saying that she would never see him again. I had that in my head for two years. I started to get the odd photograph and postcard. When he did come home, I was standing by the gang plank on the quay in Waterford and I saw this man on the plank coming towards me. I remember running and then stopping, saying to myself that this man wasn't my dad – he had white hair – but it was, the sun was after bleaching his hair and he had a deep tan. I saw his eyes and went flying into his arms. I remember him bringing home coconuts, pineapples and maltesers. We had none of those in Ireland at the time.

Anon.

A Hard Time In Life

He took over my whole life. I want to tell people, the younger people in life. People think it is only happening to you. It happened before and I had to cover a lot of it. In my experience of life, if you started being beat at the start, you take it and you make a bully out of them, your husband. It never stops. Once the first one starts, I advise anyone to do something about it. It's harder as you go through life and have kids to walk away. My kids often saw me beaten. It was very hard rearing seven children. I remember being seven months pregnant and he broke a brush off me. You hear people saying, why didn't you do something, what can you do? Years ago there was nothing you could do. It took over your life. He commanded me and put me down all the time, saying that I had nothing in my head.

I got married at twenty-two. Life was good. Wages were small. He was very bad with the money. Not receiving money was his way of keeping me down. We were scraping. He was wanting everything in life, except the responsibility. People that knew me in town were good to me. Life was good to me in other ways. As a person, I felt bad about it. I thought it was just happening to me at the time. I had put down so much time that it was very hard for me to come up. I thought I needed him. I wasn't standing on my own two feet. He made me feel that way that I had to have him there. He put me down so much that I thought I couldn't rear my kids without him.

At 58, I went to a faith healing mass with a lady in a wheelchair. I came back at one in the morning and was called all the names under the sun. I got beaten black and blue for three hours. He was drunk. I wasn't to be allowed out of his sight, go shopping on my own or with my five daughters. I cried the whole night long. I had to get away from him. The following morning I went to the Grand Parade to my solicitor for legal aid. It took me four years to be legally separated by court. I am now seven years gone from him. I have never looked back. I joined many clubs and associations. I hope my story can help someone else.

Paula O' Callaghan

Be Happy Whatever you Take Up in Life

I was born with coloboma. The pupil of the eye is not dead on centre. I have only four per cent vision. I am originally from Strawberry Hill, now living in Bishopstown. I came from a family of ten and I was the third youngest. My parents died when I was ten and eleven, Daddy died in a horrific car crash in Limerick. A year and a half later, my mother died of cancer. My sister reared us. Otherwise the youngest in the family would have been put in orphanages. We have family gatherings every so often. I have two brothers in America and one in England. We meet up on the parents anniversary, Mass and dinner.

I went to National School in Cork and then to a school in Merrion School in Dublin, which had a section for the visually impaired. I then went to Sligo to do a secretarial course. I started knitting in the early nineties with the National Council

of the Blind, Cork. I was there when the Council set up in Cork first. We make everything from blankets to clothes for Marymount Hospice and Bosnia. The Cork Council began in White Street and then moved to Connolly Hall for two/three years. We are now in Saint Mary's of the Isle Convent. It is great to meet there on a Monday morning and if you want to knit you can and if don't, you can sit down and have a chat. Noreen and Catherine in 1992 put an appeal out on the radio looking for wool and the public responded generously. I love knitting. I couldn't sit around without knitting. Today, as a Council, we could do a lot more. We need more drive. I feel that the National Council for the Blind could recognise the Cork organisation more. Dublin is not everything – we should share our resources.

Loretta Mullins McGillion

Live It!

I grew up in Queensland, Australia, spent time travelling in Europe and came to Ireland in 2000. I met my husband on my backpacking travels. I moved to Midleton in February of this year and don't know that many people, but I'm happy. I love minding my baby Liam. My first impressions of Cork were that of the cold weather, but a very pretty county. I lived in Dublin when I first came here and I have found that people in Cork are friendlier and will chat to you. I found that Dublin people stick to themselves.

I came to Ireland with the intention of not getting involved with someone. I didn't want to have a relationship across the world, but I happened to meet the right man. When it came down to living on the other side of the world without him, that simply wasn't an option.

Judith Mtifukanji

Malawian Mai in Cork

My meeting women from different cultures and backgrounds have added to my womanhood. We all have different stories but we have some things in common. We all had to leave the country that we loved and not just the country, but also our families, our friends and everything that is familiar to us. I never thought of leaving and moving far away. Coming to Cork in August 2004, I felt lost, lonely, meaningless, strange and with a sense that I am on the outside, of no use to anybody – useless. I wondered would I ever have been able to come out of those feelings, if I hadn't met people who cared enough about me to invite me out. The doctor who comes to the centre where I stayed sent me to Cois Tine. There

I was met with understanding and kindness and was encouraged to participate in the activities of the centre. I began to feel I was somebody again that I mattered. There I can talk and I can share my story. I can feel safe and have peace of mind. Without this kind of help, I wonder if I would ever have ventured out and begun to trust people again.

The women's group at the Cois Tine takes us into the wider community. At present, I am part of a group of asylum women, who with a group of Irish women, are participating in a programme, which is looking at living with diversity. I find it very helpful. We share the significant values of our cultures and gradually begin to understand and respect each other. We begin to realise that we are no threat to each other and as our conversation continues, we begin to see that we can live with difference, that I can be who I am with my culture and background and equally be fully respectful of who you are.

For us who are in the Asylum process and who spend our lives waiting for the mail, expecting every day, to get the letter, which will tell is we can no longer stay in Ireland, meetings with other women are important. We can live normal lives with normal problems. Their kindness and openness give us a sense of our normality. On the street, we can meet people who tell us to go back to where we come from and that is very upsetting. Meeting the women in Cois Tine gave me a sense of a common humanity, especially of our common womanhood. Our colour, our customs, our life experiences may be different but our basic needs for love and acceptance for family and a sense of belonging are the same.

I appreciate a lot the wonders of being a woman. I am strong, wise, determined and invisible amongst many wonders. I can be bent but not broken. I can do or face anything except bad things. I've learned that women are embryos and are still growing because they are loving in nature. They share their growing capabilities with all the human race.

The Knitting Map has made me more famous. Not only have I met wonderful women but also I have learnt to appreciate the little things that happen in life. Through our shared experiences, I have gained a lot. See me standing toe to toe, as I am spreading my heart to all women. I need to get the same. I believe in giving so as to get more. From the courage I have gained from The Knitting Map, no one can keep me down. I am strong woman from Malawi.

Valerie O' Brien

What's meant to be, Will be

My first memory as a child was the song *'I love to go a-wandering'*, which in sense summarises me as a child – I got up out of bed one morning thinking my mother was out. She wasn't and I walked in my pyjamas over Bandon Road to Glasheen. A neighbour spotted me and gave me bread and jam. I was only four.

I was born on O' Callaghan's Place and lived in Greenmount for a time. I am from Doughcloyne in Togher where my parents and Grandparents grew up. My

grandmother's sister used to run one of the market gardens in the Pouladuff area. You had to get into the city early to get your vegetables sold and make money. I remember being told stories about it. My children, Ian and Ciara were my happiest memory later on in life. They were part of me; I created them – a miracle if you look at them. I am separated seventeen years and brought them up on my own. It was very hard in the early years but they are happy now.

My interest in disability arose from a niece of mine Kate O' Brien who trained at Caritas in Sarsfield Road. I helped her a lot, but unfortunately she died suddenly on the 12th December. Months later, I read that they were looking for people at Larch. I expressed my interest. Larch is a place for adults with learning disabilities and is located in Togher. It is an international organisation, founded by John Vanier, a French man. In the Cork workshop, there is weaving, knitting, candle making, drama, art and life skills. There are five houses in the community. My work is in life skills and candles. The residents produce and sell their wares in the shop on the premises. Many residents of Larch came from Our Lady's Hospital, which had closed in recent years as well as Grove House.

Sinead Barry

Go with the Flow

I remember in Carrick-on-Suir in the garden of our house, the vegetable patch. I remember the ladybirds, the sunny day. As a teenager, life was a pain. I struggled in school due to my hearing loss. It was hard to fit in. I had to concentrate all the time to stay tuned in. I went home very tired and had to take daily naps after school. As the years have gone on, I am more positive about my hearing. I have accepted it much more. The digital hearing aids I have now are much better that what I had in school. With my hearing, I see more things as art. I love nature and animals. I attended the Crawford School of Art and afterwards got a job in Larch. It was great for me to use my talents with the residents.

Mona Lucey

Get Along with People

Blarney had two primary schools, the factory which was the main source of income for the town, a church and two pubs, post office, two hotels, Blarney Castle and of course tourists. It was a simple life. I have good memories of playing along the road. Skipping, playing house. My father Denis worked in O' Mahony's Blarney

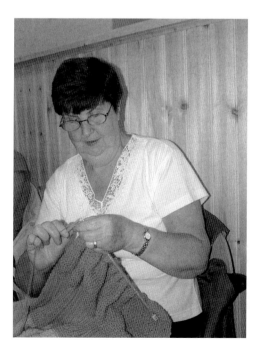

Woollen Mills and then later on as a builder. My mother Julia also worked in the Mills, but left when she had a family. She was a good homemaker and was always there for us when we were growing up. Three of my sisters (Kathleen, Mary and Bernie) and myself worked in the factory in Blarney. My fourth sister Marion worked nearby in a local shop. My brother Michael attended the North Monastery School and became a motor mechanic. I began work at fourteen in the hosiery department making socks. I left when I got married to Dan.

When I got married and moved into the city to Audley Place to my in-laws. We then bought a house on Military Road and lived there for thirty years. We settled in there from the beginning. My son was a month old and my daughter was only two. I got to know the neighbours when the kids went to school. My husband Dan died suddenly last August 2004. Coping? The days are still up and down. I have two grandchildren – Kaitlin and Connor. They're great company and I look forward to them growing up and even going through school. I am involved with Collins Pitch and Putt Club for over a decade now. Friends and neighbours are important for someone to talk to. They have been very good to come to the house and check if I needed anything, even just someone to talk to.

Kit Deeney

Kindness is the basis of life

I was born in a little village near Nottingham, but married a Corkman. I met Tony at weekly dance in Birmingham University – I was doing Social Science at the time. I had been involved in Birmingham in setting up a housing association in order to provide housing for people. I had met people in the Notting Hill Housing Association in Liverpool and we discussed the large housing problems in Birmingham. They expressed an interest in financing the first house of a proposed housing association in the city. It survived and over time, amalgamated with other association and is now called Focus Housing Association. It is now helping thousands and thousands of people in the English Midlands. That was part of one chapter of my life.

I arrived in Cork in 1966 and I was only 21. I remember that it was easy to settle in. Tony's family was very supportive. My career path changed in Cork. I had two children and got involved in assisting Maureen Black and the Citizen's Advice Bureau. It is now the Citizens' Information Centre. Maureen was a mover and a shaker, a great woman who could motivate people. If she saw a need to address a social issue, she would try to recruit the relevant resources into her network. She first of all set up the Retired Women's Association and the Citizen's Advice Bureau. After nearly thirty years, I am still a volunteer with the Bureau, which has grown to become a national organisation with branches across Ireland. I have seen much social change in Cork. In the early years, emigration was rife in the city. The issues revolved around employment rights, pension entitlements, benefits. The Bureau circulated leaflets and booklets on all those aspects. In the eighties, emigration remained and unemployment benefits were key issues, especially with the poor economy in Cork. All sorts of people would come in. In 2005, there is still a big divide in people who are well off and poorer classes. What is helping narrow the gap is access to education. People now are more confident to go out and enquire about their entitlements. I like the idea you can meet anyone on an equal social footing. I like the aspect of multi-culturalism and the integration involved.

I get huge satisfaction from volunteering. Last year, I was nominated for one of the *Irish Examiner* People of the Year awards. That was a highlight for me. I have been involved in University Hospital as a volunteer, though volunteering is on the verge of disappearing or being squashed. The status of paid work and volunteering is very different now. Initiatives developed by Volunteers are now hindered by insurance problems.

Chapter 4

Negotiating the Rhythms of Life

'I entertain myself any day walking down the street and studying people's faces – well, what is life without people? Walking down Patrick's Street is anything but bleak. Sometimes people can be very kind and giving but they can also be aggressive and domineering'. (Maura O' Connell)

Maura O' Connell

In Search of Tranquillity

I entertain myself any day walking down the street and studying people's faces – well what is life without people? If you go on a holiday to the most beautiful place in the world and you have no human contact – isn't it bleak? Walking down Patrick's Street is anything but bleak. Sometimes people can be very kind and giving but they can also be aggressive and domineering. I remember reading one time: 'rudeness is a weak person's attempt at strength'. There is logic in that. People can fascinate me but there does come a time, when I want to disappear on my own.

In 1974, my friend and myself drove to Glandore. It was my first time there. It was a beautiful heavenly place and I just adored it. I said to my friend: 'If you don't mind now, we'll stay silent for a couple of minutes. I want to try and drink this in'. I then decided to take holidays in Glandore and I couldn't get accommodation. There were very few guesthouses. On route to Skibbereen, I saw a sign on a gateway saying Sacred Heart Retreat House. We drove for a mile into the woods. It was just captivating.

A priest, Fr Smith came to the door in muffy (or normal clothes). I asked him did he take paying guest and he said yes. I went there sometime in June.

Cycling was one of my hobbies – I had a banger, a ramshackle of a car; I used to go and visit near-and-dear relatives in the country. When they passed away, I returned to my youth and bought a proper bicycle. Two guys I knew were going to Castletownbere camping and I asked them to take my bike to Myross and they did. It was pure bliss. I cycled through hill and dale. I stayed there for a week and went to all sorts of places – one day I cycled to Baltimore. It was a long distance – ten miles. I locked my bike on the sea shore and went across by Ferry. I had read that you could hire out ponies for the day and being of farming stock, I hired out a pony for the day. I managed to stay alive and dined on pony back. I went to bed tired, weary and happy and I was lulled to sleep by beautiful hymns in the distance. I discovered later that there was a body of nuns on retreat there. A few years later I went back again and have made a regular visit ever since. I feel at home there because of my long association with the place.

I like going off like that. One time I went to Jersey on a week's holiday. I went my plane and stayed in Saint Heliers and hired a bike for the week. I also went to France for a day by hydrofoil, a terrible experience.

Margaret Jones

Guiding Travels

There are positives of having a disability. Having coped with it from an early age, it made me who I was. I never hid it. When I was in my twenties, I had a very serious illness and I had my leg below my knee amputated. I had to cope with a sudden disability coupled with running a home, raising my children. That really influenced me. In due course, I started working as a volunteer in a disabled hospital firstly as a fundraiser but ultimately I went out into youth groups and schools to show that people who are disabled are not different, to educate the young people so that they would be comfortable with someone who is disabled. I used to go in as an amputee and I had a friend who had a wheelchair. It was very difficult for many children we met to realise and appreciate that the woman in the wheelchair could not get out of it and walk.

I would talk to the Brownies about the fact I was disabled. One of my great pleasures in life was knowing a Brownie who is now in her mid thirties, who went home and said that I had a wooden leg and I let us all the girls touch it. That mother was so impressed by that attitude that she joined Girl Guides as a leader. You need to be open about disability and there are different disabilities. Catherine, my daughter, worked for three years with adults who could not read or write. Those adults could not go to the shops. They couldn't read what they are buying.

They have as mush disability as I have. Other people are mentally challenging. There are people who had accident and can only move their heads. My attitude is that it happened. I am so lucky to be alive. I could have so easily died at the time. My disability has given me a positive outlet on life. I have so much to be thankful for, my two children, my grandchildren and my husband.

It annoys me that with regard to disability the difficulties people put in your way when you are disabled especially if you use a wheel chair. You could see a sign with disabled written on it. You follow it, go up an elevator and you have to go up a flight of stairs (!) or staying in a hotel and being put on the first floor.

I was born in Sheffield in Yorkshire in the North of England. I remember growing up during the war and coming home from school one day and being terrified passing the cemetery. The Germans had landed and all my friends thought that they were hiding behind the walls of the cemetery. As a child, I remember that Shrove Tuesday was an important day and all the children were given toys. The girls would get whips and tops and skipping ropes and the boys would get shuttle cocks. We played a lot of singing games such as the 'big ship sails on the alley alley-o'. I taught it to my girl guides years later.

I have moved around a lot in my life from Yorkshire to London to Vancouver Island to Ottawa to Cork. Cork – I find very complex to get around especially the narrow spaces of disability spots. I like the people in the Cork region, very welcoming. My life motto? You can do it if you try.

Clare Sands

Roar!

My name is Clare and I was named after the County of Clare because of its connection with music. I'm eleven years of age and in sixth class. My family is big into playing the fiddle. I mostly play classical music and I am at grade four at the moment. I play the bodhrán as well. I enjoy music and I think about using it when I'm older… perhaps to travel around Ireland or maybe the world gigging with my friends who play other instruments.

I came across The Knitting Map last year. My mum Sue was doing workshops with my friends and me. We were knitting scarves and it was funky knitting – in fact, she came to my school (Scoil Íosagáin in Blarney) to do a workshop with my class. I do think though that knitting is something you learn at school, have a great time doing and then when you're older you take it up again… I think The Knitting Map is cool. It has grown in size very fast over a few months.

Knitting is not one of my hobbies, I do knit the odd scarf. I do think it is great at times to sit down and whilst watching television to start knitting, sometimes I do that, but I'm the type of person who plays a lot of sport and I'm always out with my friends. What I love in life is to be active. You can't just spend loads of time in front of a play station or watching the Simpsons every single night and not getting out to see the rest of the world. My hobbies are swimming, karate and the violin.

Two years ago, I won an All Ireland cup for the Karate I competed in – that was great. I also love animals and would love to become a vet when I'm older. What annoys me in life is when I get given out to in school. Sometimes, I'm a kind of a messer. I get in trouble the odd time!

Elsie O' Connell

I had a very happy childhood

I started knitting at school at an early age. My Grandmother in Ballinguirou in North Cork raised me. The colours of The Knitting Map reminds me of the surrounding landscape where I played. My mother had me out of wedlock and left for England when I was a baby. I have to say I had a very happy childhood with my grandmother. As the years went on, I discovered who my mother was. My grandmother reared me and when I was fourteen, after my Inter Cert, I went to work in Mitchelstown. I worked in a bar for six years and I married James O' Connell from near Mallow, a great man. I had two children.

Anon.

There'll be a piece of paper that will cause a lot of trouble

A number of years ago, I went to a fortune teller with my daughter and daughter in law. During my time with her, she said there would be one document that would cause an awful lot of trouble. She told me that: 'there will a small piece of paper but you haven't got it yet'. She left it at that. I wondered was she having me on or was she really earning her thirty pounds? I came home. My daughter in law shortly afterwards persuaded me to go Lourdes with three other people. The problem was that they all had been foreign before, they all had their passports and birth certs except me. I filled in the relevant forms and went up to the Garda Barracks to get them signed. On being asked if I had my birth cert with me, I said I had none. I checked at home but I could not find it. I got to Lourdes on a disability passport I had a great time there but when I came back I wanted to get my birth cert.

I rang my mother. She did not want to know. I said I *had* to get my birth cert, especially to get an old age pension. I got my solicitor to write to my mother asking to help out. She wrote back saying that I knew who my father was. I did not know. My mother rang me a number of months later. I was watering the flowers with a teapot I had received for my wedding. She asked me if I knew who my father was. I said that I did not. She told me that my grandmother had three daughters (my mother plus two) and one son. My father was my uncle… she answered my questions. I told her I had to get my birth cert… I got it last week.

Louise Kiely

You'll Find Englishmen are Gentlemen

From rural Ireland to inner city England and back again, more or less in one piece, thank God. I was born in Inishannon and went to primary school there. Life was simple, a rural life in the 1930s and the 1940s. We were a family of nine who lived on a farm. We mostly played at home. There were more boys than girls. So I played hurling and a form of cricket. We entertained ourselves. We were lucky to have a battery radio. My home is still there and my nephew is living there with his wife and children at the moment.

I went to Bandon Secondary School and then to Boarding School in Millstreet, Co. Cork. I was eighteen when I went to England. I had tried to become a nun. I really wanted to become a missionary but I was told by the priest that I was not strong enough for that life. I studied a correspondence course to achieve my A levels and then attended Exeter University, studying French and Latin. I liked the city very much and was very happy there. I started teaching first in Torquay

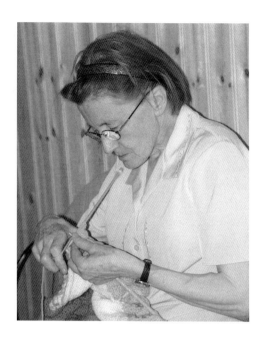

and taught there for six years. I came back to Ireland for a time, but returned to England to teach in Cornwall, Dorchester and Hull. All the early schools I taught in were private schools. The schools at Hull and Withersea were comprehensive. I found the change quite challenging. There were smaller classes in the private schools compared to bigger classes in the public schools. I found it exhausting, but always had something funny to tell at lunchtime.

I was very happy in England. Everyone was kind to me and supportive. That was my experience. My father was an Irish patriot and had grown up in a period of civil war. Strangely enough he said to me when I was going to England, 'you'll find Englishmen are gentlemen'. I must say I found his statement to be true and it helped me a lot when I was living in England. I often meant to ask him what he meant by it especially with his involvement in national matters in Ireland. In fact, I can't think of one Englishman I knew who was not a gentleman.

I came back to Cork in 1981 and did post office work in Dennehy's Cross. My motto in life is: face it because I think that's all you can do. There are moments where you'd love to run away but you can't. I have now 'pitched my tent' on Kilbrogan Hill in Bandon and live a secluded life. I am a very tense person and I work hard. I think I would feel lost if I was out and about in society today. It is a very different society... there are more opportunities for young people nowadays. My favourite prayer on my life journey is the hymn by Venerable Cardinal John Henry Newman, it is called *Lead Kindly Light*. Now, in the final stages of my journey, I find the last verse particularly encouraging:

'So long thy power hath blest me,
Sure it still will lead me on,
O'er moor and fens,
O'er crag and torrent till the night is gone,
And with the morn,
Those angel faces smile,
Which have loved long since,
And lost awhile'.

Lionel Powell

Striving to Improve Self

The colours of The Knitting Map are wonderfully Irish. We have very subtle colours in Ireland. Our colours are not as strong as the continent. I really like the way it sweeps down from the Knitting Station. I was in Australia for a number of months and when the sheep are shorn. The sheep go out a chute, like a knitting station and its wool flowing. The map flows like the lovely River Lee.

I'm from Sunday's Well on Strawberry Hill. I remember as a child with my pals getting any sort of four wheeled device, going up to the top of the hill and flying

down. You veered left onto the flat at the Women's Gaol. We were very lucky as kids as we had ponies. I remember getting presents from relatives in Nash's Boreen and hacking home but the pony got faster and faster, came down Hollyhill onto Blarney Road – very scary but exhilarating stuff. I held on for dear life.

My love of art grew over time. I had open minded parents. If you tried something, they would encourage you. I got the freedom to try different things. I evolved well that way…well grounded. I was originally a builder by trade. I did a short course in art in Venice years ago; I got a scholarship for four months. There were really good teachers. I was taught how to draw and opened up the art work.

I worked on restoration projects in the US for ten years, initially with a firm and them with others. I began to take courses on art and figure modelling and then focussed on decorative plaster. I did many of the classes in the hope I could use the skills I learned if I ever returned to Cork. Cork used to be a very frustrating place to live but now it is a lively place for artists. I came home in 1997 from the States. What struck me about Cork when I came home, I can recall coming through Sunday's Well past Wyse's Distillery and picturing the city centre as one large covered mall. It was something I encountered in the US, large covered shopping malls.

Cork is an amazing County to be in. The free things here are priceless. You are so close to the sea that you can tap into it at any level canoeing to yachting. The countryside is free. I grew up on the edge of that, tapping into the resources. Overall, Cork has really improved in the way attitudes are becoming more open. There are people clinging on to old attitudes. It's not good for you. My motto is can do, it's a great habit to get into. I think we're here to be tested. You can get better all the way through life. You can strive to improve self.

With art and architecture, we have one architecture college, which in Dublin. The training is all or nothing. Ideas are not spread about the countryside to those people building homes. There are very few structures in place to bring people with an interest in architecture on. It took me twenty years to get me where I am. You gradually get there to become a very useful person in the community. There are no courses that bring people softly through an architectural education. Our architecture is only adequate. It could be fantastic. If it were better we wouldn't be bored with the monotone houses we have at the moment.

Margaret O' Sullivan

Everything Really is Larger than Life

Years ago in primary school in Macroom, Co Cork, I had loved knitting so I went along to have a look at the Knitting Map. Like everyone who visits I was encouraged to knit a few rows and I just kept coming back. I'd recommend

knitting because clothes you knit yourself are so unique and with knitting getting fashionable again, there are so many modern patterns and yarns available. When I'm not knitting or working I love travelling. I used the long summer holidays during my four years at U.C.C. (studying Biomedical Science) to travel in Europe and America. Some of the places I've been are, London, New York, Washington, Prague, Budapest, Vienna, Warsaw, Berlin and Barcelona.

It's hard to pick a favourite because I've loved different places for different reasons. New York was amazing because it's so familiar from films and television and when I got there it was exactly as I expected it to be. Everything really is larger than life. I can't imagine you'd ever run out of new things to do there and of course, there's the shopping! Berlin was interesting because it's so steeped in history, I wouldn't normally be very interested in history, but in Berlin you're so surrounded by it that it becomes interesting. I remember following the path of the Berlin Wall around the city and being amazed at how it divided in two what are now main streets.

While in Eastern Europe, I had an opportunity to visit Auschwitz. Very little, if anything, has been changed from its original layout, probably just enough to make it safe for visitors. All of the staff are relatives or descendants of people who died there. It sounds like a very difficult job for them to do but they say that it's a valuable opportunity to inform people of what happened there.

I've enjoyed travelling so much because I've met people from different parts of the world and it really does broaden your mind. Sometimes I've been reminded of how fortunate we are in this country, other times it's just a chance to lie in the sun for a few days and the next holiday is always something to look forward to when life is getting you down. Recent terrorist attacks have made me nervous about travelling but I do hope to visit more countries in the future. I've enjoyed being involved with The Knitting Map and all the conversations I've had with the lovely ladies I've met there.

Nokuthula Nkomo

We Talk … We Find Out About Different Cultures

My name is Nokuthula Nkomo and I come from South Africa. I arrived here on the 26 September 2002. I arrived in Dublin to escape the abuses of my family. It was difficult for me. It was very cold and I did not bring enough clothes with me. I applied for asylum. They told me they were transferring me to Cork and I arrived in Kingston accommodation centre in Cork in January 2003. This month they told me I did not have a place to stay. They said I am just signing in and not staying there. I told them that they have never come to see me sleeping there. They did not give a nice offer. I called the Department of Justice and told them all the helpful activities

I am involved here in Cork especially Cork City Partnership and Cois Tine (an asylum forum) where I heard from Sue Tector Sands of The Knitting Map. I used to knit in my country and the Map was important for me to join. The Map has not only given me more knitting skills but I have also met helpful and interesting people. I am very proud to be part of the Map. The Cois Tine Project with Dr Agnes voiced for me to stay in Cork and to stay with The Knitting Map and the other local projects I am involved with. In Cois Tine, we receive counselling, we talk, we find out about different cultures. The cultures between Ireland and Africa and within Africa are so different. Cork is now my home and my future. I wish to help each other in similar situations as myself and to create a brighter future.

Marilyn Munza

Believe in Yourself

My motto in life? Believe in yourself; don't worry what other people think of you, you are the only one that matters. I am from Namibia and I came to Ireland two and half years ago. I have a baby boy Deo and my husband is Deogratias. The biggest change in my life is when I had to leave my country and my family. I found it difficult to deal with culture in Ireland especially the attitude to black culture. It

was a turning point in my life to adjust to fit in. I arrived into Dublin and then was sent to Cork by the asylum claim office two weeks later. They treat people very bad. My first impressions of Ireland were horrible. People were very racist. They treated me like a nobody. Gradually though I have learned that everyone is not racist.

When I came to Cork, I still had it in my head that people were bad. It took me two years to realise that not everyone was. My son was born here and I want to bring my child up here. It's difficult to establish a life and a home. I decided to work at NASQ at reception and with Cois Tine and meet Irish people on the ground. That's how I made a life for myself, by getting out of the house by doing volunteer work. I am not allowed to work. My hopes are I can remain in the country – and that my son Deo will be the first black president of Ireland! I would love to be in a position to change attitudes, black people are not bad…

Marie Foy Twomey

A Walk in the Countryside

I got into poetry when I was eight years of age. I used to lie out in the garden in the summer and my mother used to put on the record player. I used to try and write the words of the song with my pen and I reckon that's what trained my brain to write poetry. You know, songs are very like poems. When you're writing poems,

if you get writer's block, you should visualise what you have written. I used that technique for my poem, *A Walk in the Countryside*. I visualised myself getting off the bus from the city and meeting a dog barking at the gate – the mind must be part of the story you're writing.

I never knew I could write poetry until my poem was read out on 96 FM and I won a hundred Euros for it. Alice Taylor has published a few poems for me, as well as the annual *Hollybough*, *Ireland's Own* and the *Muskerry News*. I've had a few published and I am thinking of putting them into a book – you have to take the risk. If you write a poem it can go either way for you; you can be rejected and a rejection is very hard to take. I never wanted to be a poet but a writer. I bought all these books; *Writing for Television*, *Writing for Radio*, *Writing a Novel*. I wrote a novel years ago *Forgive me Darling* but it remains unfinished…

I was reared near Rocklodge Pitch and Putt in Muskerry and I was brought up in a cottage next door to the course. I got into knitting through my mother who knitted morning, noon and night. She used to make us hold out our hands holding the wool while she wound it. You could be holding out your hands for a couple of hours! We moved from Rocklodge to Ballincollig and then I went to Boarding School in Kinsale. I worked in a factory and at Saint Finbarr's Hospital in the baby unit where my child was later born.

I'll tell you a story. I was also involved in guiding, we went out to the Isle of Mann and we had a big troop of girls with us, twenty or thirty girls. We went up by boat and stayed in an adventure park; it was called Leahy's Farm, outside Ramsey. As kids do, they jump around and this child jumped off a bunk bed and badly sprained her ankle. We were going on a trip the next day to Douglas. The kids were going swimming and all excited and we couldn't leave the girl at 'home'. The best thing to do was to put our motto into use, be prepared. So we decided to make her wooden crutches. We measured her and left her off to get the feel of them. They didn't fit exactly so we made two more sticks and carved pieces on the wood so that the sticks could slot in under her arms. She wasn't very good at balancing and we bandaged up her shoulders, but anyway we went off down to meet the tram. The tram was very narrow to get about but we got on and a voice was heard: 'what about me'. The girl with her crutches was too wide to get in the door of the tram. We couldn't turn her. We had to cut the bandages off and wait for the next tram – we were not expecting that to happen but it did happen.

Another story concerns my daughter's first day at school, she came home roaring crying and I said: 'Denise what happened to you?' I thought someone might have given her a dig or something, she said: 'No, Mammy'. She sat in the hall, with her head in her hands. I said: 'Something must have happened' and she replied: 'Mammy, the teacher asked us whose mammies bake and I put up my hand and said you that you bake scones – but you don't bake nothing'.

The Knitting Map
By Marie Foy Twomey

Purling through the main streets,
Cables for the paths
Cork city is created
And knitted as a map.

Vibrant in its making,
A pleasure to the eye,
Captures the heart of the city,
The core of human life.

Cameras that are placed
High above the city,
Gather the information
That keeps the knitters busy.

Everything from weather
To street and population
Through computer technology
Go through transformation.

For hour after hour,
people knit together,
To make the knitting map
A treasure forever.

Maureen O' Sullivan

A Poet's Escape

I am an avid fan of G.A.A. and poetry. When I was young my brother would always be reciting it and took an interest in it. My husband died six years ago and just to take away the thought, I picked up poems and started learning them. I must explain this poem to you first, one of the first I learned. I picked it up in a magazine a few years ago. There was this man and he was doing a line with a girl and they parted and he decided to compose a poem about her.

My darling Kitty
I think you're pretty,
In town or city there in none like you.
I really love you and the sky above you,
But since you left me, I'm feeling blue.
Your Aiken dress and stylish dresses
Give my heart a treat.
In the gloaming, I go roaming around Bandon
And the Convent Hill.
In the glowing ember, I do remember.
When November was cold and wet,
You'd stroll so simple around the temple where we often met.
In every weather, we'd pull together.
That we loved each other, there was no doubt.
You once confided you were undecided
And we got divided it was a bad knockout.
Right off, I started to plough new ground.
I searched the city for one like Kitty,
I was a pity, none could be found.
I met with lassies, all types of classes
With gowns and sashes down to their feet.
But I'd go at random to get back to Bandon
And meet you in the North Main Street.
To conclude this ditty, it is into Phelans.
I will make a call and we will start all over
And be in clover and together.

Rita Guinan

I'm their number one fan

I'm the number one fan of Westlife and I have all their autographs, photographs, books and CDs. My favourite is Nicky Byrne. He sings a lot of songs on the albums. I went to their concerts in Lansdowne Road, the Point and Millstreet. My favourite song is *I Believe in Angels* and my favourite album is *A Kick in the Head*. I have many posters on the wall at home.

I like knitting. It makes me calm and relaxed. I'm from near Neptune Stadium and was brought up in the fifties. The people know me and I know them. I have one brother Raymond and one sister, Mary. My mother passed away a few years ago. I miss her. I follow Na Piarsaigh. My brother used to play with them years ago.

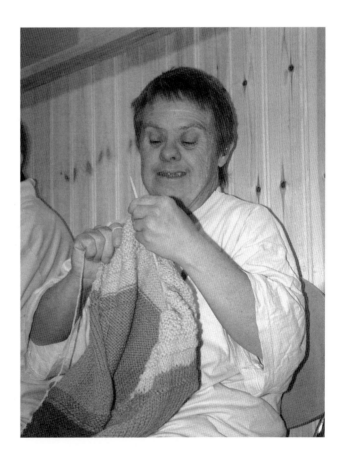

Samantha Barry

Everything Happens For a Reason

Within three months, I seemed to belong in Dublin. I didn't feel out of my element and Drumcondra became my new home. When I'm based somewhere, I like to feel that I am meant to be there and I like the feeling of stability. I don't have my old home in Cork and it was important for me to feel at home in Dublin. People are different there, if you are a Cork person in Dublin and you meet other Cork people – there is that instant 'I think you're cool – I like you because you're from Cork'. If you were at home down south, they might not be your favourite person in the world! There is a sense of anonymity about the capital. When you go out in Dublin, you can go to a different club or pub every night and you will never see the same people again, unless you want to. In Cork, you're constantly running into people you know.

I like living in Dublin and I didn't think I would as much as I do now. I have great friends – a network of people who I have met over my years in college and through work. While a lot of my friends are true Dubs there is a rivalry between Cork and Dublin people. Dublin people do find issue with the 'People's Republic of Cork'. Roy Keane's autobiography opens with 'Cork people have a chip on their shoulder' and that is one statement that you get thrown in your face a lot. Thankfully, most of the Dublin- Cork rivalry is friendly banter.

Coming back to Cork, I fall in love with the city again within minutes of walking down Patrick's Street, looking around and seeing what has changed. I love the kind of memory that Cork brings back to me. One thing that Dublin lacks is the Cork sense of humour. We are just born funny people. The men are different, they don't chat you up in Dublin – men in Cork are not afraid to chat you up while you're out. Many Dublin guys – and I know this a sweeping statement, which I suppose I shouldn't make – but they do think they are brilliant and they don't approach girls. They think they are too good for you and they don't bother. It's the girls that do all the work in Dublin whereas in Cork, you have a fifty-fifty chance.

I'm originally from Ballincollig and when I finished my degree, I went away for a summer to New York. When I came home I didn't have a proper job and I decided to move to Dublin. It was a spur of a moment decision. During a drunken phone-call with a friend of mine Melanie from my U.C.C. days she suggested I moved in with her in Dublin. Within three days I had packed my bags and got a job. I had never really visited Dublin before, so everything was different. When I moved, my parents moved to Bantry. So my home – well home was not an option anymore. So it was all or nothing. I decided to give the place a try for six months and it was hard. The people I lived with were from Tipperary and Limerick and

they went home every weekend. I made a promise to myself that I would try to stay in Dublin and make friends. That was not the easiest option in the world to take. However I met many friends through a girl in work who I got to know and I'm still quite close to.

Radio is very important to me. I always remember listening to the radio when I was younger, listening to the Top Forty Countdown. I never thought I would be a radio journalist but I absolutely love my job. I love news and I can't get enough of it! Even when I come home in the evening, I check the news channels to see if anything has happened since I came off the bus! I find I don't have time to read all the news I want to read! Recently, I was in Bantry and coming back up that morning, I was listening to the radio through my phone on the bus, about ten o' clock and I heard about incidents in the London transport system and reports of a bomb. I began to get phone-calls from friends at work and in Dublin asking what was going on. I had to get another bus from Cork to Dublin but I was really frustrated that I couldn't see what was going on the telly. Reaching Dublin, I felt like a real journalist. It was awful to watch and hear how the events unfolded – you do feel sympathetic but there's something about a major news story like the London bombings that gives you a rush, you know how important it is to get the story out to the general public who want to know.

I love my job but working in the news has made me very cynical. I write the news for Radio One and 2FM and you're working to an hourly deadline. If you're in a newsroom and something happens in Iraq, it's not newsworthy enough unless a large number of people have died, but one person dead in Cork and Dublin and its news for one or two days…

Cynthia Kelly

Don't Take Life Too Seriously or You'll Never Get Out Alive

I was mad about him for years. He was good looking and I had high expectations. I always go for the intelligent ones. It was my last year, Grade six and it was time to leave. At the end of year party, we met up down the back of the hall —he nearly mauled me. I nearly died, he was smothering me, I'll never forget my first kiss for as long as I live. I'll be telling my grandkids about it. I still kind of liked him though afterwards, the guys I go out with must be funny and they must know what they want in life. It wrecks my head when they don't know what they're doing, but I am stubborn at the best of times. People who can't make up their mind annoy me, fussy people, people who think they are higher than everyone else.

I'm seventeen and originally from Fairhill and went to school in England for ten years. There are differences between there and Ireland. The people were weird but not in a bad way, teenagers over there are different – you have a set group of friends who you have to stay with, where here you can mix. They have a very different sense of humour.

I came back to live in Cork last year and it was hard to settle in. Coming back, I felt that I missed out. The young people in my area had gone to school with each other and had got to know each other quite well through the years. I felt like an outcast. The city had changed so much by the time I came back. I used to remember where every alley was in Blackpool but many of them are now gone, many of the old buildings have been knocked down. We do need new buildings but knocking down old buildings that can be repaired is just wrong. We shouldn't try to make Cork look like every other European City – it is special in itself. At the moment I do shop and craft skills in Gurranbraher-Knocknaheeny Training Centre. I would like to pursue a youth and development course in Saint John's College, Cork. I'd also like to travel, but my favourite place in the world is home.

Sue Tector-Sands

This Ain't no Dress Rehearsal, This is the Real Thing

I was born into a family of craftsmen, all my family work with their hands and make a living from it. We were also very self-sufficient growing up and this way of life taught me to very resourceful to this day. My grandmother taught me to knit when I was five, my other grandmother to crochet and my mother to sew. It is to these three remarkable talented women that I dedicate this year to. These three women have now evolved into my three daughters – Clare, Tiarna and Lainey.

I moved to Cork twelve years ago and at first found it extremely difficult to fit in. I had a three-week old baby. My husband Seamus was away a lot and I knew no one. My first memories of Cork are of being very lonely. I also found the Cork people cliquish and still do to a certain extent. They have so many of their own family around that they have little time for blow-ins. I also found it very isolating as I did come from a very large extended family. If truth be said, I was envious of them. To me family is everything in life. However, time moved on and as my children got older and started school, other blow-ins became my new family and today, we are well settled.

I started working in the Gurranabraher and Knocknaheeny Training Centre ten years ago as a training instructor in home management. The centre is a FÁS community training centre to cater for early school leavers. I always taught the adult group. I love working on the northside of Cork. I believe there is a very apparent

divide between north and south of the river. I find northsiders sound. I love their humour, their friendliness. They are forward and say what exactly is on their mind. They really have no inhibitions and I admire that in people. I have worked with my many groups in the northside over the last number of years, in particular Niche, Mná Na Feasa, Education Rights, Ógra Corcaigh. I am full of admiration for the work they do. However, with teaching, I began to feel burnt-out – you need a lot of motivation and energy to keep ahead of our young people today.

I then got the opportunity to run workshops for The Knitting Map. I taught six different workshops. I wanted them to reach a diverse bunch of people. I started off teaching knitting to thirty ten year olds in Blarney Girls School and then to Niche (Northside Community Health Initiative). Workshops also took place at to the National Institute of Training and Development where I taught young people with physical and mental disabilities, then at Gurranabraher-Knocknaheeny Training Centre, Colaiste Choilm and transition-year students and then finally onto Cois Tine and Sister Mairéad's asylum seekers. The young people also used their participation as part of the community section of their Gaisce President's Award. All the groups are still involved in The Knitting Map. I have also continued to run workshops during the year in Saint Luke's Hall doing knitting, crochet and most recently, a children's textile summer camp.

In January 2005, I took a leave of absence for a year from my job to work on The Knitting Map full-time. This year has been a marvellous revelation to me. I've fallen in love with Cork! What a fabulous city we have. I really feel like 'yes, we have arrived'. I love what European Capital of Culture has done for us. The feeling of anticipation when you're waiting for the next Corcadorca performance, the lively discussions over coffee about some play the women of the Map have seen in the Everyman Palace, the buzz around the city and all the colourful foreigners. I love that it has brought art, drama and cappuccinos out on the streets and of course our very own Pied Piper! There is so much happening and it annoys me when I hear some moaner on radio saying: 'there's shag-all on'. I mean what stone is he hiding under?

As for The Knitting Map, I've met some other amazing people You never know who's going to walk in the door – a street band from Trinidad, Pakistani Sailors, two Rasifarians who do street art in Patrick's Street, the list is endless. To me coming from a community background, The Knitting Map was always going to be about community. The textile artists – and they are artists – we've met on the Map are amazingly talented women, weavers, spinners and lace makers. It has been my privilege and delight to work alongside these women, the exchange of gossip, ideas, patterns and knowledge has been invaluable. I sincerely hope that the legacy from this year is that we can continue. I would dearly love to see this space retained as a centre of excellence for textiles in Cork.

My summary of life? Without being too melancholic, three or four years ago, I found a lump in my back. I had to have surgery. It turned out to be nothing. When you have a scare like that, it gives you a wake-up call. My motto has really come into play: this ain't no dress rehearsal, this is the real thing. In other words, live life to the full... I hope to do so.

Cork 2005 Team

The Box over the Bed

Tom McCarthy

To me, there were two aspects of The Knitting Map that were compelling – the sheer scale of the project, ambitious in its imagination and conception and ambitious in its dreams in what it might mean at the end of the project. The other compelling idea was that the Map was an unselfish work of art. It opens out to so many people. As a writer myself, the making of most art is achieved through the process of aloneness. The Map is where the artist looks out and tries to bring others into the making of art – a concept and the fulfilling of a dream.

Historically, The Knitting Map to me is also an important reminder of the importance of women's work. I remember that during Cork 800 a fantastic anthology was brought together by the Cork Women's Poetry Circle; it was called *The Box Under the Bed*. That work, which would be considered women's work, was visible to the public eye and in many ways the story of women's action in the city was anthologised. When that small anthology was published, it was attacked in the press. It was actually mocked. The Knitting Map, twenty years later, has also been subject to attack. It interests me about Irish and Cork society that when women's work is made visible, it somehow attracts negativity from sources in the media. Why is it that women's activity attracts negative feeling in the media? It seems like we have come from *The Box under the Bed* in the mid 1980s to The Knitting Map, perhaps 'The Box Over the Bed' in the twenty-first century?

Mary McCarthy

The Knitting Map is an artistic-technology project as well as a community development project. It has brought people together from different parts of the city and county, many of whom have not been connected before, from different backgrounds and different cultures. The Map has also brought the participants

back out into society for various cultural events over the last two years. It is an accessible art form but also incredibly beautiful and valued by its knitters. It has been a huge leap of faith as no one initially knew what would be created. The process of bringing people together has been essentially for two years. The Map is a driver of creative energy – all the knitters are all artists in their own right. The Map is a hopeful project and it is very heartening to see so many people dedicate so many hours of their time of their own free will to the Map.

Tony Sheehan

Cork 2005 commissioned The Knitting Map because it was a very interesting and unique fabric and technology project. We were particularly interested in the way that the map looked at the literal and abstract aspects of the city. It has grown to become a very strong community development project, not by accident but as part of the Map's evolution. As there are so many people involved from the knitting community who created the work through their craftsmanship, it has created a great social centre and a great sense of purpose. It also gives access to people who are not ordinarily involved in cultural aspects in their lives.

Appendix One
Stitch Patterns and The Knitting Map
(*halflangel,* 2005)

1.   Garter Stitch
2.   Stocking Stitch
3.   Reverse Stocking Stitch
4.   Moss Stitch
5.   Irish (double) Moss Stitch)
6.   Moss ZigZag Pattern
7.   Basket Weave 4 by 4
8.   Basket Weave 6 by 6
9.   Reverse Stocking Stitch Check
10. Large Basket Pattern
11. Large Honeycomb Pattern
12. 1 by 1 Rib
13. 2 by 2 Rib
14. Wide Rib
15. Garter Ridge Stitch
16. Lareg Garter Stitch Ridge
17. 1 by 1 Cable
18. 8 Stitch Cable
19. 6 Stitch Cable
20. Ladder of Life Cables
21. Honey Comb Cable
22. Open Honey Comb Cable
23. Wavy Cable
24. Diamond and Moss Stitch Cable
25. Big and Little Cable
26. Interlocking Stitch

Appendix Two:

Rainbow of colours that represent a range of weather

(*halflangel*, 2005)

Colour 1 (Technology decides)	Or Colour 2 (Technology decides)	Range of Weather (1-26)
128 Dusky Rose	No choice	26 Wet and blustery, stormy
Dusky Rose	Nutmeg	25
Burgundy	Plum	24
Burgundy	Dusky Rose	23
Eucalyptus	Ivy	22
Ivy	Indigo	21
Indigo	Plum	20
Plum	No choice	19
Devon Blue	No choice	18 Medium, probably wet
Devon Blue	Heather	17
Heather	No choice	16
Heather	Amethyst	15
Amethyst	No choice	14
Lavender	Devon Blue	13
Putty	Devon Blue	12
Putty	No Choice	11
Sandstorm	Ivory	10 Bright but not so warm, still-ish
Storm Cloud	No Choice	9
Storm Cloud	Sandstorm	8
Sand	No choice	7
Glencoe	Ivory	6
Khaki	No Choice	5 Bright, still and warm (Summer)
Khaki	Putty	4
Putty	Lavender	3
Amethyst	Lavender	2
Putty	No Choice	1
Stone	No Choice	5 Bright, still and warm (Autumn)
Stone	Biscuit	4
Sand	Naturelle	3
Sand	Biscuit	2
Sand	Cinnamon	1

Other titles published by Nonsuch

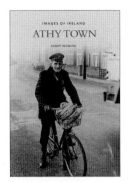

Images of Ireland Athy Town
ROBERT REDMOND

Athy is a sizeable and fast developing heritage town in County Kildare with a rich history dating back to the 12th century. Robert Redmond is a well established photographer and has taken photos all over County Kildare and Athy in particular. There are wonderful and varied pictures featured in this book – social, religious and sporting events are illustrated, not to mention, the people and picturesque landscape of Robert's much loved town.

1-84588-502-3

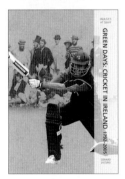

Images of Sport Green Days: The History of Irish Cricket
GERARD SIGGINS

Irish cricket has a long, colourful history. The earliest photo of an Irish team is an 1858 team group of the Trinity 2nd XI – cricket was by far the most popular and widely played game in the country until the foundation of the GAA in 1884. At its height in the mid–1880s there were 98 clubs in Tipperary alone, by the 1970s there were none. Designed to appeal to the casual and the hard core follower this book is a must for Irish Cricket fans.

1-84588-512-0

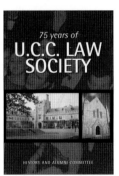

75 Years of U.C.C. Law Society
HISTORY AND ALUMNI PROJECT COMMITTEE

U.C.C. Law Society has had a varied and interesting history. Informative and entertaining, including archive photographs and pieces by guest writers, this book outlines the changes, controversies and history of the Law Society since the 1920s – from its origins as a society for the educated elite to an active college society, organising charity, educational and social events. 75 Years of U.C.C. Law Society will interest law students and alumni as well as those interested in Irish social history and the history of Cork.

1-84588-513-9

The Uncrowned King of Ireland
KATHERINE O'SHEA

This book, first published in 1914, provides us with the greatest insight currently available into the love life and political story of Charles Stewart Parnell. Katherine O'Shea, gives an account of their passionate romance and a slice of the political intrigue and machinations of the era. Contianing many heretofore unread personal and political notes, telegrams and letters, The Uncrowned King of Ireland offers an incredible cache of primary resources to historians and those interested in Irish politics generally.

1-84588-534-1

If you are interested in purchasing other books published by Nonsuch, or in case you have difficulty finding any Nonsuch books in your local bookshop, you can also place orders directly through our website
www.nonsuchireland.com